"There are few people who understand and have given more to America than Allen West . . . so when he shows his concern for the direction of Texas, we should all pay attention. His research and solutions make this a must-read for anyone who bleeds red, white, and blue."

—BRIAN KILMEADE
Cohost, *Fox & Friends*; host of *The Brian Kilmeade Show*;
New York Times best-selling author of *Andrew Jackson and the Miracle of New Orleans*

"Texas is under attack! Fill the sandbags, and dig the foxholes. Lt. Col. West delivers the strategy, insight, and "everything's-bigger-in-Texas" attitude to defend the conservative government ideology that built our beloved Lone Star State."

—SAM MALONE
Morning show host, AM 1070 The Answer, Houston, Texas

"Everything's bigger in Texas . . . including politics. *Hold Texas, Hold the Nation* is Allen West's powerful commentary on continued success in the Lone Star State."

—TOM DELAY
Former Republican Leader, US House of Representatives

"As an American and a Texan, I am thrilled to hear anything Allen West has to say about maintaining wise, conservative government for our state and our nation. Few have walked his path as a military hero, a member of Congress, and now a valuable private-sector writer and thinker. Allen West is an American treasure."

—MARK DAVIS
Talk show host, Salem Media Group

HOLD TEXAS, hold THE NATION

HOLD TEXAS, HOLD THE NATION

VICTORY or DEATH

Lt. Col. ALLEN B. WEST (Ret.)

BROWN BOOKS
PUBLISHING GROUP

Hold Texas, Hold the Nation
Victory or Death

Brown Books Publishing Group
16250 Knoll Trail Drive, Suite 205
Dallas, Texas 75248
www.BrownBooks.com
(972) 381-0009

A New Era in Publishing®

Names: West, Allen, 1961-
Title: Hold Texas, hold the nation : victory or death / Lt. Col. Allen B. West
    (Ret.).
Description: Dallas, Texas : Brown Books Publishing Group, [2018] | Includes
    bibliographical references.
Identifiers: ISBN 9781612542980
Subjects: LCSH: Texas--Economic policy--21st century. | Texas--Economic
    conditions--21st century. | Conservatism--Economic aspects--Texas.
Classification: LCC HC107.T4 W47 2018 | DDC 330.9764--dc23

ISBN 978-1-61254-298-0
LCCN 2018954913

Printed in the United States
10 9 8 7 6 5 4 3 2 1

For more information or to contact the author, please go to
www.TheOldSchoolPatriot.com.

I dedicate this book to my dear lovely wife,
Dr. Angela Graham-West, and our daughters,
Aubrey and Austen, for whom I fight and defend
their life, liberty, and pursuit of happiness.

CONTENTS

PART 1: THE BATTLE FOR TEXAS'S SOUL

1. "COME AND TAKE IT!"
   A Call to Arms..3

2. IDEOLOGIES AT WAR
   Conservatism versus Progressive Socialism 13

3. TEXAS VICTORIOUS
   Success the Size of Our State...33

4. THE DECLINE OF LIBERALISM
   Why California Is Always a Seller's Market 65

PART 2: NO SURRENDER

5. THE FRIENDLY STATE
   A Tax Code That Pays...85

6. LIVE AND LET LIVE
   Minimal Regulation 101

7. SOUTHERN HOSPITALITY
   Probusiness Policies 135

8. UP BY THE BOOTSTRAPS
   Social Policies That Empower the People...........................147

CONCLUSION 167

ACKNOWLEDGMENTS...181

ENDNOTES 183

ABOUT THE AUTHOR 205

PART ONE

THE BATTLE FOR TEXAS'S SOUL

CHAPTER 1

"COME AND TAKE IT!"

A Call to Arms

Attention all lefties! Join DSA NTX at QueerBomb 2018. QueerBomb is Dallas' only LGBTQ2IA+ celebration that happens during Pride month, featuring no cops and no corporations! Our Queer Socialists will be tabling starting at 7:00 PM, with the rally and performances planning to start at 7:45 PM and the big march starting at sundown! Come live your queer fantasy with us; the dress code is wear whatever you want as long as it's red. Bring signs, flags, drums, whips . . . really whatever you want to express yourself and queer solidarity. All are welcome.

—Facebook post, June 23, 2018[1]

Solidarity with everyone in the #ICEOutof PDX Coalition, including our Portland Democratic Socialists of America comrades!

#AbolishICE #Not1More

—Facebook post, June 25, 2018[2]

Join us at our interest group's next meeting, as we
discuss build [*sic*] on our priorities, roles, and current
issues.

—Facebook post, June 26, 2018[3]

Looking at these Facebook posts, one might assume they belong to
an organization in some progressive socialist state on either one of
our coasts. Given that they're inviting "comrades" from Portland,
one might guess that the organization is on the West Coast, perhaps
in California. But these posts, in fact, are copied directly from the
Democratic Socialists of America North Texas chapter, proudly
recruiting under the tagline "Y'allidarity." At the time this book was
written, they had 2,144 followers.

It might seem incredible to imagine socialists in North Texas,
that bastion of capitalist growth. North Texas, she of the Dallas, Fort
Worth, and Arlington metropolitan area that in March 2018 boasted
a 146,000-resident jump from 2017, the most of any metro area in
the United States.[4] In fact, six of the top ten fastest-growing counties
in the United States were also in Texas, including Tarrant, Dallas,
Denton, and Collin counties.[5] For each year between 2010 and 2016,
Texas has had the nation's largest annual population growth. During
this period, the state added about 211,000 people per year through
natural increase.[6]

Good old-fashioned conservative capitalism has taken Texas to the
top. "The most likely reasons people relocate to Texas are its resilient
economy and relatively affordable housing," Texas state demographer
Lloyd Potter at the University of Texas at San Antonio observes. "Oil
and gas production continues to be a major component in the state's

economy, but other sectors such as information technology, manufacturing and biomedicine are important sources of job growth."[7]

Texas's characteristic conservative capitalism has carried it from infancy to the world's tenth largest economy—independently of the rest of the United States of America. With a gross domestic product of more than $1.6 trillion, it's ahead of Canada, Korea, Russia, Australia, Spain, and Mexico.[8]

Characteristics are different from traits. Characteristics refer to those distinctive qualities that make up an individual. A trait, on the other hand, is the inherited feature of an individual. Texas's sheer size, great weather, central location, and bountiful natural resources of bubblin' crude—oil, that is; black gold; Texas tea—are traits. You can't hate on traits; just stand in awe of them. It's equivalent to being born with tall parents, a strong jawline, and a fat trust fund.

But the state's characteristics enabled her to succeed even when her traits failed. Texas weathered the oil slump last year through employment gains in other industries, such as leisure and hospitality, where jobs grew 3.5 percent from 2015 to 2016. We added a total of 210,200 jobs over the course of the year.[9] "We also have a vibrant economy that offers employment opportunity to a lot of people up and down the spectrum," said James Gaines, chief economist at the Real Estate Center at Texas A&M University, in a March 2017 *Dallas Morning News* article, "from low income to high income, from low tech to high tech."[10] Among the fastest-growing occupations in Texas are web development and several in health services, according to the 2014–24 state projections. Web developer jobs are expected to grow by 37 percent over that decade.[11]

The Threat of Political Calculus

Texas is clearly thriving. With its exploding economy and rapidly growing population, it may seem obvious that Texas policy is doing something right. But what the progressive socialist left sees in Texas is not its incredible success. What they see is an opportunity for continuous national electoral power. It all comes down to the vital political calculus of Texas.

In order to put this into a clearer perspective, we must break down the electoral college by state. The United States has 538 electoral votes in a presidential election cycle, and it takes a majority of 270 electoral votes to win. Those electoral votes are calculated by a presidential candidate winning a particular state.

As a result of the 2016 presidential election, the left is not exactly a fan of the electoral college because their calculations failed them. But the electoral college operated just as the Founding Fathers desired—they did not want the most populated states to dominate national level elections. So, when the Democrats complain about Hillary Clinton winning the popular vote, that is because she won the most populous states. However, she failed to hold the states that have these past few years made up the "blue wall." Like Jericho, it fell when working-class US citizens deserted her for now president Donald Trump, swinging their states red.

The strategy of the liberal progressive left in America has been to go into successful red states and flip them based upon flooding the major urban centers. That has been the case with Colorado, which was once a solid red state that went purple and now, due to the cities of Denver and Boulder, is a blue state.

The left has attempted the same strategy elsewhere, like in North Carolina and Virginia.

Their strategy has been successful in Virginia, where the dominance of government employees in Northern Virginia has altered the political landscape of the state that gave us many of our first presidents and the authors of our Declaration of Independence and Constitution.

Electoral politics comes down to winning certain designated states.

A list of the major, double-digit electoral states:

California	55
Texas	38
New York and Florida	29
Pennsylvania and Illinois	20
Ohio	18
Georgia and Michigan	16
North Carolina	15
New Jersey	14
Virginia	13
Washington	12
Tennessee/Massachusetts/Indiana/Arizona	11
Wisconsin/Maryland/Minnesota	10

Just so you know, Alaska, Delaware, Montana, North and South Dakota, Vermont, and Wyoming all have only three electoral votes each. Needless to say, there are not a lot of presidential political ads airing in those states. But what is obvious to anyone is why, even with businesses and individuals moving from failing leftist states, the left has their eyes on Texas.

If the progressive socialist left can replicate what they have done elsewhere, taking over major urban population centers, they feel that even Texas can one day be theirs. It is easy to ascertain that if the left were to ever achieve winning California, Texas, New York, Florida, Pennsylvania, Illinois, Ohio, Michigan, New Jersey, Virginia, and Washington . . . Well, you get my point. Texas's proud history of successful conservatism is at risk, and we must fight to protect Texan success.

Why Am I Writing This Book?

Wait a minute, some may ask: Why is ol' Colonel Allen West writing this book? Is he even Texan? Why does he care about the Lone Star State?

It's true: I'm proud to say I grew up in Atlanta, Georgia. My first introduction to the Lone Star State was as a young boy sitting with my dad and watching the 1960 classic *The Alamo*, starring John Wayne, Richard Widmark, and Laurence Harvey. I was always a geek when it came to history and loved to read and study about critical battles. I was simply enthralled with men who would make a stand for freedom. Men who would lay down their lives for something greater than themselves. Men who would sacrifice for a cause that would define the present and set the conditions for future generations. Men who would stand against seemingly insurmountable odds, even knowing their eventual demise was coming.

Ever since that day, the Lone Star State has reminded me of the other stars that have been used as guiding lights—the Star of Bethlehem, which the wise men followed to find our Lord and Savior Jesus Christ, and the North Star, which sailors used for navigation millennia before GPS.

That Alamo stand on March 6, 1836, has always been a similar beacon for me. It reminds me of the simple maxim my mom instilled within me: "A man must stand for something, or else he will fall for anything." When Colonel William B. Travis drew that line in the sand, it was a real commitment, a true honor to stand. The second they all made the decision to fight, they were victorious. The Mexican forces killed Travis and his men, but not the movement. Victory or death. As for me, I will stand for conservative values and conservative success until the end, and I will make my stand in Texas.

"Come and Take It"

Spartan king Leonidas, a man on my list as one of the greatest military leaders, made a similar stand. Liberty stood before tyranny in a far-away place, on a narrow pass at the "hot gates" of Thermopylae in 480 BC. Liberty was in the form of the Spartan personal guard of Leonidas and a few other Greek city-states who answered the call to arms. Tyranny was presented in the form of Xerxes and his massive Persian horde, which had returned to the Hellespont vowing to subjugate all of Greece. On that very first day of the Battle of Thermopylae, Xerxes demanded of the Spartans to lay down their arms. Leonidas replied with two simple words: "*Molon labe*." Those words have a definitive meaning for America and Texas. The translation is a bold statement: I double-dog dare you to "come, take."

More than twenty-two hundred years later, in 1778 at Fort Morris in my birth state of Georgia, that same rallying cry was echoed: "Come and take it." And the defining moment, the spark that created the Texas Revolution, occurred on October 2, 1835, when the Mexican cavalry ordered the Texians at the town of Gonzales to return a small cannon. They replied: "Come and take it." On my inner right forearm there is a tattoo of two words in Greek: "Molon labe." Those two words symbolize my life, one of taking a stand for liberty against tyranny.

After learning the story of the Alamo and later enrolling at the University of Tennessee, I became even closer to Texas. I am, and forever shall be, a Tennessee Volunteer, and I know the history from which our moniker comes. I had to educate one clueless fan during the 1988 Peach Bowl in Atlanta. My Volunteers were playing Indiana University, and I asked an Indiana fan, "What is a 'Hoosier'?"

He responded that it came from the phrase "Who's your neighbor?" I recall scratching my head. Continuing the conversation, he asked me who the Volunteers were. With extreme pride, I retold the story of the Tennessee volunteers who went to Texas to aid in the fight against the tyranny of General Santa Ana. These great men were led by Davy Crockett, who famously stated upon losing his congressional reelection, "May you all go to hell; I am going to Texas." I told the Hoosier fan about how these men stood and fought to the end at a place called the Alamo and that, later, it was students from the University of Tennessee who volunteered to join the army in the Mexican War. There were a few Georgians amongst that group also. I told them about Sam Houston, the first president of the Republic of Texas, who had been a governor of Tennessee and a member of Congress from the Volunteer State. The Hoosier was amazed at the history . . . and probably frustrated that Tennessee won the game, 27–22.

Since living here in Texas, I have become great friends with former Dallas Cowboys football star Jay Novacek. He constantly reminds me of how they used to beat up on my Atlanta Falcons. It was always the Dallas Cowboys who were "America's Team" when it came to football. No matter where you went in America, you saw that Lone Star, that symbol on the helmet of the Cowboys, which is what we have come to know about Texas.

I guess it was fitting that my final duty assignment in the US Army was at Fort Hood, Texas, in the Fourth Infantry Division. I will never forget that very special day, June 6, 2002, the sixty-eighth anniversary of D-Day, when I assumed command of a field artillery battalion in a division that had landed on Utah Beach on that famed "longest day." Our little family fell in love with Central Texas and Texas Hill Country. I remember getting my Texas driver's license and feeling a very special sense of pride. Having spent a good deal of my army career in the Midwest, Oklahoma, and Kansas, I loved being able to wear my jeans and boots, my favorite attire to this day.

I moved permanently to Texas in December of 2014 to accept a job offer at a public policy foundation, and I couldn't be happier. I stand with the many who claim the old mantra "I may not have been born in Texas, but I got here as soon as I could!"

Over my years in Texas, I have traveled extensively through the Lone Star State, and I've realized what makes it special. From the rolling pine tree hills of East Texas, out to Amarillo, down to the Gulf coast of Corpus Christi, and out to Midland and Odessa, to the Guadalupe Mountains, the high altitude of El Paso, down to Marfa (yes, I saw the Prada display case) and the Big Bend Mountains, to Del Rio along the Rio Grande and San Antonio—whether in my Jeep Wrangler or riding on my 2016 Victory Cross Country 8-Ball motorcycle—I've seen why Texas is worth fighting for.

People are still following that Lone Star to Texas. In Texas, there is a true sense of pride, honor, and victory—not a bunch of people standing around feeling like victims. But tyranny, in the form of the collective subjugation of the progressive socialist left, is once again attempting to invade Texas. They demand Texans lay down all that defines them. They demand that the men who enabled Texas to be what it is today—Sam Houston, Stephen F. Austin, William B. Travis, Davy Crockett, James Bowie, Mirabeau Lamar—be forgotten, as the cities that carry some of those names are not reflective of the principles and values for which they fought.

Our enemies are not clearly defined. Socialists rarely wear T-shirts and ballcaps identifying their allegiance. Americans everywhere tend to follow the social graces and keep controversial topics hidden. We're adept at sidestepping landmine topics of politics and religion until we're assured we're around like-minded souls.

We fight a complicated war against wayward minds that only vaguely reveal themselves in the form of coded hashtags and Facebook pages, impromptu restaurant meetings and YouTube videos, and ultimately on Election Day for local, state, and national offices. But I refuse to let progressive socialists take our Texas. The spirit of those two words from 480 BC lives on: "Molon labe!" Come and take it!

CHAPTER 2

IDEOLOGIES AT WAR

Conservatism versus Progressive Socialism

It can be easy to reduce the war of ideas happening today to a war between Democrats and Republicans, "blue states" and "red states" on an electoral map on the television. But the labels of "Democrat" and "Republican" represent different ideologies than they did fifty years ago. Believe it or not, from Texas's early days through 1976, it voted for Democratic presidential candidates. Texas Republicans didn't start controlling state-level positions until the 1990s.

But even though Texas's political affiliation changed over the years, the state's ideology really hasn't wavered in its more than 170-year history. That's why it's more accurate to view our nation's politics in terms of prevailing ideologies. If you limit your focus to simple labels—such as Democrat and Republican—you'll miss the core argument being debated throughout history.

Ideological Differences

The central argument is over prevailing ideologies of how voters view the role of government in their lives. Conservatives believe it is better to have less government, minimal taxes, and local control over state services. Progressive socialists support bigger government, and they're willing to increase taxes to create parity among the people.

Put another way, it's about equality of opportunity versus equality of outcomes. Conservatives believe in protecting everyone's opportunity to succeed. Progressive socialists believe that government is responsible for ensuring outcomes are fair, in a system where everyone is rewarded the same.

There are many problems with equality of outcomes. For starters, the concept of "fairness" is subjective. Progressive socialists will continuously create new regulations and laws in an attempt at making life fair. Alexis de Tocqueville, a nineteenth-century French political scientist, coined the term "soft despotism," which describes the state into which a country overrun by "a network of small complicated rules" might degrade. Soft despotism gives people the illusion that they are in control when in fact they have very little influence over their government. Tocqueville warned that soft despotism—the kind wielded by progressive socialist officials—breeds fear, uncertainty, and doubt in the general population.

In *Democracy in America*, written in 1840, de Tocqueville writes that soft despotism "does not destroy, but it prevents existence; it does not tyrannize, but it compresses, enervates, extinguishes, and stupefies a people, till each nation is reduced to nothing better than a flock of timid and industrious animals, of which the government is the shepherd."[1]

Pure Government

It would be a mistake to assume that conservatives are against all laws and forms of government. In broad, simple terms, conservatives believe that law should enable people to defend themselves. We have the right to defend—even by force, if necessary—our lives, our liberties, and our properties. And people should be permitted to combine their rights and organize a common force to provide a consistent defense of their lives, liberties, and properties. That's what I call government.

This type of government has a reason for existing: to protect individual rights. Just like it would be unlawful for an individual to take the life, liberty, and property of another individual, it should be unlawful for the government to destroy the life, liberty, and property of individuals. No one in their right mind would claim that they have a God-given mandate to annihilate the rights of another man and woman. Likewise, the collective force, or government, can't claim to have this right.

If ever there were a nation founded on a simple platform like this, it could be a model for the world to follow. Citizens of this hypothetical nation would feel assured they had an administration defending their personal safety and the fruits of their labor from domestic and foreign attacks.

If, by chance, a few of those citizens became more prosperous than others in the nation, they would not feel pressure to thank the government for their success. Conversely, the government would not think it necessary to levy higher taxes on those who were more prosperous in an attempt to create parity among its citizens. The government's responsibility would be to simply ensure the blessing of safety. If this government continued to stay out of private affairs, the wants and needs of the nation would satisfy themselves in natural order.

The United States of America was founded on that simple principle. The men who drafted the Declaration of Independence made a simple commitment to defending its citizens' life, liberty, and pursuit of happiness. Throughout history, when those rights were in jeopardy, men and women fought valiantly to protect them.

Unfortunately, over the years, our laws have done more than simply provide the blessing of safety. As French economist Claude-Frédéric Bastiat wrote in 1850, law has been perverted through "stupid greed and false philanthropy."[2] For example, laws enacted in our nation's history to sanction slavery and dehumanize groups of people were wrong and were rightfully abolished. Conversely, laws that punish people for good fortune and honest prosperity, just to fund the lifestyle of less fortunate citizens—or those who choose not to work as hard—are also unjust.

We have fallen victim to enacting laws that create an exaggerated importance on human passions and our political struggles.

Texas Conservative History

From its earliest days, Texas has been a proponent of the conservative governmental ideology: the line of thinking that believes government should protect individual rights. For years, Texas was Democratic but still staunchly conservative. The state has always pushed for smaller government, lower taxes, and local control of services. People here have never liked being told what to do, especially by some bureaucrat up north.

Texas's economic prosperity started with the role the state's architects decided to play—chamber of commerce instead of welfare office. When government plays the part of chamber of commerce, it zeros in on removing barriers to growth and getting out of the way of natural supply and demand forces. But when government plays the role of welfare office, it passes rules to "protect" citizens and shepherds social programs, which inadvertently—and sometimes advertently—place a heavy yoke on employers, who are society's best wealth creators.

The fiscal conservative principles that made Texas great were born underground. Around the mid-1920s into the 1930s, miraculous oil discoveries instantly turned poor Texas families into millionaires. Attention quickly turned toward protecting this newfound wealth. And nothing threatened their lifestyle more than president Franklin Roosevelt's New Deal initiatives, which were knee deep in taxes, federal financial oversight, and costly labor protections.

Texas historians point to John Henry Kirby, owner of the Kirby Lumber Company, as the grandfather of Texas conservatism. At one time, he owned more pine acreage than any other man in the world, according to Bryan Burrough's research in *The Big Rich: The Rise and Fall of the Greatest Texas Oil Fortunes*.[3] In the 1920s, Kirby created the Houston Oil Company, which held his oil rights. However, he lost his wealth in the Great Depression and was bankrupt by May of 1933. His ire turned toward President Roosevelt. He funded organizations to challenge the New Deal—Texas Tax Relief Committee, the Texas Election Managers Association, the Sentinels of the Republic, the Southern Committee to Uphold the Constitution, and others. It was all an effort to prevent Roosevelt's reelection in 1936. As we know, Roosevelt still was reelected and Kirby died in 1940, but he kicked off a movement.

By 1938, oil-backed ultraconservatives took control of the state's political culture, according to George Norris Green's book *The Establishment in Texas Politics*.[4] Kirby's heir apparent was legendary oilman Hugh Roy Cullen, who funded several conservative initiatives, and most notably helped support the election of W. Lee "Pappy"

O'Daniel for governor. During the primary, his opponents promised government handouts, but Pappy ran on the platform of the Ten Commandments. He defeated the other candidates and eliminated the need for a runoff.

After the attack on Pearl Harbor, Roosevelt increased federal oversight over the local economy. Cullen and other oilmen stepped up the pressure with funding opposition on a national level. At the end of a 1942 *Washington Times-Herald* advertisement against Roosevelt, Cullen said, "The people of Texas do not want a dictator . . . And if you fail to pass proper laws to control a possible dictatorship—while our brave boys are fighting to preserve democracy—then you should resign at once and permit patriotic men to take your place, so that our children may enjoy the blessings of freedom!"[5]

Those oilmen who didn't necessarily label themselves as conservative were definitely still probusiness and formed Washington alliances to make sure Texas business interests were secured.

The Great Political Migration

Though Texas was Democratic through and through, it still had a two-party system of moderate Democrats and conservative Democrats. Any Texas politician wanting to get elected had to run as a Democrat; it was the only option.

Texas became a state in December 1845, participating in its first presidential election in 1848. Texas seceded from the Union in 1861 and was not included in the 1864 or 1868 elections. From 1872 through 1976, Texas went Democratic in the vast majority of elections. However, that changed in 1980, and Texas has sided with the Republicans ever since.

Texas essentially broke up with the Democrats when the party left its first love. The Democratic party gradually shunned its conservative roots. The party started taking up social causes that made conservatives uncomfortable. Both parties moved away from the center. The Democratic party became more socialist, and the Republican brand became a defender of conservatism.

Democrats became more of a welfare state. In 1977, president Jimmy Carter's Community Reinvestment Act inserted the federal government into the mortgage industry. The result was the creation of toxic subprime mortgages and government-sponsored hotbeds of mismanagement such as Fannie Mae and Freddie Mac, nefarious financial practices resulting from the repeal of the Glass–Steagall Act, and finally a financial meltdown in 2008.

Many notable Texas Republican leaders used to be Democrats. Phil Gramm, an economics professor from Texas A&M University in the late 1960s through the 1970s, started as a Conservative Democratic politician, but he switched parties in 1983 and ran for the US Senate as a Republican. Rick Perry was elected as a Democratic member of the Texas House of Representatives in 1984, serving three terms, and even worked as a state campaign organizer for Al Gore's presidential campaign in 1988. He switched parties in 1989.

President Ronald Reagan, a transformative president in our nation's history, was once a Democrat, but he switched in 1962. "I didn't leave the Democratic Party," Reagan famously said. "The party left me." The party left a lot of people.

Like most of my family, my parents, Herman and Elizabeth Thomas West, were registered Democrats. Regardless of party affiliation, I was raised with very conservative principles and values. Conservatism in the black community was not so much about political inclinations as it was a way of life. In 1908, Kelly Miller became one of the first scholars to draw the connection between the black community and conservatism in his essay "Radicals and Conservatives."[6] Miller, who was the first black scholar to graduate from Johns Hopkins University and later served as dean of Howard University, classified followers of Booker T. Washington as conservatives.

In the black community, conservatism is rooted in individual liberty. That follows the ideology of John Locke's classical liberalism. I've said this before, and it's worth repeating: Who better to seek true freedom and liberty than those who suffered under the yoke of slavery? If America and the dreams of the Founding Fathers were to have any meaning, slavery had to be abolished. Once it was, the blessings of liberty would have to be secured for those who hadn't previously enjoyed them. I firmly defend my position that black conservatives have always seen individual liberty as the prerequisite true justice, not government-manufactured economic or social justice.

It is interesting to look at how the political parties have changed in just the last twenty years, from Bill Clinton's first election as president in 1992 to Hillary Clinton's failed election as president. In studying data from the Pew Research Center, the Democrats' demographic rapidly transformed into a group of voters with more progressive socialist views on issues like gay rights and immigration. The Republicans have dramatically shifted toward issues of limited government and defending the right to personal security, emphasizing the Second Amendment.[7]

California's Shift

If Texas is an example today of a conservative state, California could be considered the definitive example of a state married to the progressive socialist ideology. "More than any other pair of states, they stand as proxies for the national debate about the size and shape of government and which direction a divided America should go in the future," writes Dan Balz, chief correspondent at the *Washington Post*.

California was not always a progressive socialist state. California has a conservative history as old as Texas's, but while Texas kept its conservative roots as political parties changed around it, California has drifted in a different direction. A couple of factors steered California toward the path of progressive socialism. Immigration, especially from Latin America, played a big role in the 1980s and 1990s. These immigrants and their children were more likely to side with Democrats. Republican efforts in 1996 to cut off illegal immigrant access to certain public services were eventually overturned by the courts, leaving a negative image in the mind of many Latino voters. Latinos now make up almost 40 percent of the population, wielding enough power to basically block conservatives from statewide office, according to a March 27, 2017, analysis from *The American Interest*.

Since it entered the Union, California has absorbed tens of millions of Americans from other states, including most famously during the Gold Rush, the Dust Bowl, and the postwar era of Federal investment and industrialization. But as the state turned blue in the 1990s, the pattern reversed. Patterns of outmigration over the past twenty-five years due high taxes, unaffordable housing, and overregulation have drained California of its conservative constituents.

In 2010, the state passed a law requiring candidates to participate in a single consolidated open primary, often called the "jungle primary." In these primaries, the top two vote-getters end up on the election ballot, where they square off against each other. This system has driven many Republicans off the election ballot, as the top two slots are often won by Democrats.

Some Republicans originally backed the jungle primary law, including then governor Arnold Schwarzenegger. They hoped it would help moderate candidates in elections and thus make the state more bipartisan.

But what has happened is the exact opposite. This law made California ripe for one-party rule.

As the Daily Signal's Fred Lucas wrote in *The American Conservative*, it led to bizarre absurdities, such as Democratic senator Dianne Feinstein being labeled the "Republican" option in a Senate race due to the fact that her only opponent was a more militant progressive than her.[8]

Real political challengers are simply drowned out by the number of progressive voters in these primaries, and so a single ideology with only minor variance gets represented in the general election.

Larry N. Gerston, a professor emeritus of political science at San Jose State University, wrote for the *Los Angeles Times* that the jungle primary not only wiped out the Republican Party in California but wiped out third parties that previously could challenge the status quo.

"California reformers argued that the major parties were dominated by extremes on the left and the right, and that a top-two system would attract centrist candidates, especially in districts where one party was dominant," Gerston writes. "They also contended that more competitive races would increase turnout. Early studies show that neither expectation has been met."[9]

In addition to the one-sided jungle primary system, a redistricting plan in 2010 tightened Democrats' grip on the state. Initially billed as a nonpartisan effort to do away with gerrymandering, the plan was hijacked by state Democrats, who stacked the commission with progressive activists posing as "Republicans."[10]

This further wiped out opposition to the Democratic Party in the state over the last decade.

Richard Fisher, the former president of the Federal Reserve Bank of Dallas who served from 2005 to 2015, gave a speech at a luncheon on November 15, 2012 at Stanford University entitled "The State of the West."

In his speech, Fisher challenged the audience on their state's troubled trajectory. "The question is: Why? Why has the Golden State lost its luster and become a place where the economic burdens of its people have become hard to bear, when once it was the very exemplar of happy, hearty dynamism that is the West?" Fisher asked. "How could it be that the hardscrabble Lone Star State has come to replace California as the engine of the West's economic growth?"[11]

Wealth Redistribution

The answer lies in what the philosophy of equality of outcome does to the heart and motivation of a people. When a citizenry is obliged by the government to give up its earned benefits to others, when businesses are burdened with overregulation and heavy taxation, their ability, their very initiative to create wealth, is slowed.

Even in California, the most famous founders of the Silicon Valley startups and technology companies have stymied others with the ways they break free of the philosophy of progressive socialism as it is usually defined in this way. Gregory Ferenstein, a veteran tech journalist for *Fast Company*, summed up the confusion this way: "A lot of writers have scratched their heads trying to classify Silicon Valley's unusual politics, calling it 'quasi-libertarian' and 'peer progressivism.' Back in the '80s, a tech-obsessed faction of the Democratic party called themselves 'Atari Democrats.'"[12]

Ferenstein polled 129 Silicon Valley founders about their belief systems. Here's what he found:

Most tech founders belong to the Democratic Party, with 83 percent of employees at top tech firms giving money to president Barack Obama's election campaign in 2012. Forty-three percent of startup founders self-identify as Democrats—while 31 percent don't identify with any political party.

However, the company founders tend to be Libertarianish in practice. Nearly all of them claimed, in some form or another, that they are apolitical technocrats who just want the government to get out of their hair while they build products that solve problems much better than bureaucrats ever could.

They believe all problems are information problems. "It's the hacker ethic that a lot of problems in the world are information inefficiencies," wrote Facebook's founding president, Sean Parker, in response to Ferenstein's survey.

But what should be most telling for city officials is how these tech founders feel about interdependence. According to Ferenstein's survey, these tech founders often criticize a "zero-sum" view of the world. "Most economic fallacies derive from assuming there is a fixed pie, that one party can gain only at the expense of another," tweeted Google chairman Eric Schmidt.[13] That tweet may sound familiar—it's a quote from conservative economist Milton Friedman.

The tech founders of Silicon Valley don't believe in equality of outcome but, instead, equality of opportunity. They see mediocre economic growth as a bigger problem for broad prosperity than discrepancies in wealth. "I believe if we have 4 percent a year of GDP growth, all these problems would get solved," said Paypal cofounder Peter Thiel.[14]

The tech founders' honest beliefs about equality are hard to extract, Ferenstein said.[15] These company leaders often skirt the issue by talking about equality of opportunity instead of equality of outcome. But equality of opportunity is not some social contract ethic about what people "deserve" to earn if they're successful; it's about maximizing people's contribution to society.

So Ferenstein asked them a more difficult question: Is meritocracy naturally unequal? In a perfect meritocracy, one in which income is distributed exactly in proportion to one's contribution to society and everyone has an equal shot at being successful, what would the economy look like?

One hundred percent of the tech founders to whom he presented this question said they believe that a truly meritocratic economy would be "mostly" or "somewhat" unequal. This is a key distinction: opportunity is about maximizing people's potential, which founders tend to believe is highly unequal. Founders may value citizens' contributions to society, but they don't think all citizens have the potential to contribute equally.

Founders also prefer competition among public services. This helps explain why tech elites like Bill Gates and Mark Zuckerberg have given hundreds of millions of dollars to charter schools, which happens to be a conservative-led idea to improve education that teacher unions hate.[16]

Even business leaders in California know that wealth redistribution and widespread government-led services are a recipe for failure.

Destructive Policies

In Claude-Frédéric Bastiat's 1850 essay *That Which Is Seen, and That Which Is Not Seen*, he presents a story of a hoodlum who is believed to be creating prosperity by breaking windows of a shopkeeper. Money the shopkeeper spends to replace the windows is now circulating in the local economy, and a new job of replacing the windows is created. Bastiat argues against this type of prosperity by destruction. He instead makes a case for what would have been produced had the windows not been broken. Perhaps the money the shopkeeper saves from not having to replace a window is invested back into the business, or he buys new shoes for himself, or something else.[17] The overall message is that far too many of our government policies and regulations break windows, and we've been led to believe that the business of repairing and replacing them is sufficient. The regulation and taxation progressive socialists endorse to ensure equality of outcome for American citizens "breaks windows" and costs money our people could use to create more prosperity on their own—and make their own decisions about how to pursue their happiness.

Here's a real-life example. I remember questioning Cass Sunstein, president Barack Obama's regulatory czar, while I served on the US

House Small Business Committee. Sunstein was testifying before us when he made the statement that more regulation was good for job growth.

We asked him to explain what he meant. He responded by saying that when you have more regulation, you have to hire more people to enforce the regulation. Huh? That's a thuggish business model: breaking windows and making the owners of the shop pay you to fix them.

Whenever a law or regulation is passed, good or bad, it creates a series of effects. There's always an immediate intended impact of a regulation that everyone can see, but there are other unseen effects that unfold in succession.

This is a fundamental difference between the two prevailing ideologies battling it out in Texas and across the nation. The short-sighted economic policies of progressive socialists—promising to give constituents stuff with little to no strings attached—will focus on the immediate visible effect of a regulation or law. The wiser economic policies of conservatives will take into account the hidden impact of that regulation or law. What typically happens is that while the immediate consequence of a regulation is favorable, such as free health care for everyone, the ultimate consequences are harmful, perhaps even fatal. The shortsighted economist pursues a small present good, which is followed by greater damage. The wiser economist pursues a greater good, even though there's a risk of a small present damage.

The Young Socialists

But across the nation and now in Texas, progressive socialism is gaining adherents. Right now, Facebook Inc. cofounder Chris Hughes, thirty-four, is proposing a plan for the government to give a guaranteed income of $500 a month to every working citizen earning less than $50,000 a year. Hughes estimates it would cost $290 billion a year.[18]

"Cash is just the simplest and most efficient thing to eradicate poverty and stabilize the middle class," Hughes said according to Bloomberg's May 4, 2018, report.[19] His idea is being trumpeted by the Economic Security Project, a major recipient of his philanthropy.[20]

Forget breaking windows; if Bastiat were alive, he would argue that we've now blown up the whole bleeping store, but many young Americans, passionate and compassionate but inadequately educated on the background to this ideological battle, are more and more in favor of policies like Hughes's, which seem at first glance to promote security and prosperity for all.

My question is, at what point do the payments end? What's stopping a future Democratic candidate from proposing monthly payments of $550? What about $600? Just make it a straight $1,000, or a "stack" or "kilo," as the young folks say. In fact, you could simplify the process and install a drive-through window at the two US Bureau of Engraving and Printing facilities in Washington, DC, and Fort Worth, Texas. Fresh, crisp Benjamin Franklins just waiting for you to pick up. But the money has to come from somewhere.

According to recent research from the Victims of Communism Memorial Foundation, the majority of millennials now want socialism over capitalism.[21] The results are unsettling, to say the least. The millennials who would prefer socialism to capitalism is a full 10 percentage points higher than the general population.[22]

That's a troubling sign for a state like Texas, which has one of the nation's youngest populations, with a median age of less than thirty-five years. I would not be surprised if the Democratic Socialists of America North Texas chapter becomes one of the nation's largest chapters in a few years.

But what's also telling from the survey from the Victims of Communism is that an overwhelming majority of millennials couldn't offer a correct definition of socialism.[23] Most young people have no idea of its deadly ties to Karl Marx's ideology and how it gave birth to people like Mao Zedong, Leon Trotsky, Vladimir Lenin, and the Kim and Castro families.

There's room for education, but we better act fast. We may lose the war before our enemy even knows what they are fighting for—and when they have won, they are certain to regret it.

President Lincoln clearly understood the nature of progressive socialism and how it would give rise to those men who all had a per-verted definition of liberty and advocated for tyranny instead. Lincoln argues that the world has never had a good definition of the word liberty.

"With some, the word liberty may mean for each man to do as he pleases with himself, and the product of his labor; while with others the same word may mean for some men to do as they please with other men, and the product of other men's labor," Lincoln said at a speech in Baltimore, Maryland on April 18, 1864.[24] I know I will always stand for the first definition—the conservative definition—and against the right of a progressive socialist government to impose upon the historical rights and privileges of Americans.

False Claims against Conservatism

If there is confusion in young people today about the end and defi-nition of progressive socialism, however, there is also confusion about the end and definition of conservatism—confusion progressive socialists promote at every opportunity. In Texas and the nation's struggle against the socialist welfare state, progressive socialists argue that we're weak on social services and that we put business interests above humanity. Not true.

First, we must never underestimate the importance of a job. There's a reason conservatives focus so much on creating jobs: they are the sources of income and the root of security and wealth for a productive people. Without income, a person cannot consume and invest, engaging the driving engines of economic growth. Most importantly, a job is the route to dignity as we have historically defined it in America.

Second, we must remember that economic growth is the foundation for the other goals and aspirations a society may have.

"You cannot pay for social services unless you have the tax revenue to do so," said Fisher, the former Federal Reserve Bank of Dallas president. "You cannot have tax revenue unless you have sources from whom to collect it. And the best revenue source of all is a citizenry that is fully employed and an economy that is prosperous. Moreover, we must not forget that a job is critical to a sense of self-worth, dignity, and pride."[25]

Progressive socialists claim their very name proves that they are the forward thinkers of the nation, while conservatives are living in the past. I say that if conservatives are living in the past, we are living in the past only in the sense that we still believe in freedom from an interfering government. We want the same classical liberalism of John Locke. We want a government to simply defend our individual freedoms, our pursuits of life, liberty, and happiness.

It is progressive socialists who are living in the past when they promote tired socialist thinking with a push for free college, free health care, free money, and guarantees for this and that. As we will see, none of this is conducive to a successful, forward-moving society—but rather to stagnation, uncertainty, and corruption.

Yet senator Cory Booker (D-NJ) is proposing to give fifteen local areas federal money so they can promise jobs to people.[26] In April 2018, Booker announced the Federal Jobs Guarantee Development Act, which would create a three-year pilot program in which the Department of Labor selects up to fifteen local areas and offers every adult in that area at least fifteen dollars an hour, including family/sick leave and health benefits. Seriously?

"The federal jobs guarantee is an idea that demands to be taken seriously," Booker said in a statement. "Creating an employment guarantee would give all Americans a shot at a day's work and, by introducing competition into the labor market, raise wages and improve benefits for all workers."

But according to estimates from the Center on Budget and Policy Priorities, the plan could cost in the neighborhood of $543 billion per year.[27] That's almost as much as Medicare's $707 billion annual budget or our defense budget of $622 billion.

If you listen closely, you'll hear hoodlums breaking glass windows.

University of California Berkeley economist David Cord published a white paper with colleagues at the Institute for the Study of Labor and found that these so-called active labor market policies "have negligible, or even negative program impacts at all time horizons."[28]

Conservatives believe we have the right to pursue our happiness. Progressive socialists like Senator Booker believe they can guarantee happiness.

Booker isn't the only progressive socialist pushing guarantees. Of course, it wouldn't be a socialist discussion unless senator Bernie Sanders (I-VT) can have a say. Sanders is actually going a little further and wants a plan to guarantee every American a job at fifteen dollars an hour, if they want it. According to an April 23 *Washington Post* article, Sanders's jobs guarantee would fund hundreds of projects throughout the United States aimed at addressing priorities such as infrastructure, caregiving, the environment, and education. Under his job guarantee, every American would be entitled to a job under one of these projects.

"The goal is to eliminate working poverty and involuntary unemployment altogether," the *Washington Post* quoted Darrick Hamilton, an economist at the New School for Social Research. "This is an opportunity for something transformative, beyond the tinkering we've been doing for the last forty years, where all the productivity gains have gone to the elite of society."[29]

Agreed. It's definitely transformative—toward socialism.

Proponents of the plan trace the idea back to the New Deal era, when President Roosevelt pitched a "Second Bill of Rights" to Congress in 1944. First on Roosevelt's list was the "right to a useful and remunerative job."[30] Talk about old thinking.

But in addition to the dangers of progressive socialism—represented in societies that have gone to the farthest extremes—it doesn't even work. Studying the examples of Texas and California presented in this chapter in more depth shows the true end of the conservative and progressive socialist ideologies.

CHAPTER 3

TEXAS VICTORIOUS

Success the Size of Our State

A miracle is defined as an event not explicable by natural or scientific laws. My Lord walking on water—miracle. His healing of the blind, deaf, and lame—all miracles. Dr. Angela Graham-West marrying this ol' Southern boy—a sho 'nuff miracle.

Our state's success, however, is not a miracle. The "Texas miracle" phrase caught fire in recent years, but pull back the curtain for a closer look. You'll see hard-fought conservative principles giving birth to business ingenuity. That's Texas.

Not only can this success be explained, I'm going on record to say it can be emulated.

Texas benefits from low taxes, a fair legal system, and leaders who know how to close a deal with incentives. That business savvy continuously creates jobs in industries like technology and energy. It doesn't take a Milton Friedman mind to understand how removing barriers to business growth is a good thing.

Texas ranks in the top five in every major study of the best states for business.[1] *Forbes* magazine ranks the state number two overall behind North Carolina.[2] It ranks number three in favorable business costs, number two in growth prospects, and number one in economic climate.[3] More than one hundred of the nation's thousand largest public and private companies are based in Texas.[4] In addition, the Kauffman Foundation says startup activity in Texas is the strongest among larger states.[5]

But that's just from the economists' and policy wonks' viewpoints. What about the CEOs, those who are actually running companies? According to *Chief Executive* magazine, CEOs nationally routinely rank Texas as number one on its annual list of the best and worst states for business.[6] The rankings were based on chief executives' perceptions of states' business climates and took into account several key measures. According to the most recent report, Texas led the country in exports last year, shipping more than $230 billion in goods.[7] Texas also has the second-largest state airport system and more miles of freight rail than any other state.[8]

In the survey, Texas continues to take the top spot in technology, retail, energy, manufacturing, and financial services. It ranked number two, trailing only Florida, in both health care and pharmaceuticals/medical products.[9] Now folks, that's diversity.

It has definitely helped us keep unemployment low. The state's unemployment rate reached an at least forty-year low of 3.9 percent in November 2017.[10]

Texas arguably has the most diverse economy in the nation. You no longer can define Texas as merely an oil and gas state. Sure, Irving, Texas–based Exxon Mobil Corp. is the world's largest oil company, but Texas is also home to the world's largest airline, world's largest automaker, world's largest telecommunications company, nation's largest homebuilder, and others.

Texas Is a Technology Leader

Hollywood enjoys putting Texas in a box of being lucky, oil-drenched savages who are technologically inferior to the progressive socialist left's coastal genius. But the truth is that our conservative principles and innovative thinking enabled us to leverage oil, clearing a path for amazing technological discoveries.

Take, for example, the formation of Geophysical Service Inc. in 1930. John Clarence Karcher and Eugene McDermott created the company to use refraction and reflection seismology to explore oil deposits. During the 1940s and throughout World War II, the company produced submarine detection devices. In 1951, the company was renamed Texas Instruments, with Geophysical Service as a division, which was later sold to Halliburton in 1988.

This new company, Texas Instruments, developed the world's first commercial silicon transistor and transistor radio in 1954. Then it invented the handheld calculator in 1967. Every few years or so, it came out with a new discovery—including the single-chip microcontroller in 1970; the digital light processing device in 1987, which makes your movies so cool to watch; and the graphing calculator in 1990.

Texas's history of technology leadership doesn't stop there. The Lone Star State practically invented the modern personal computer business back in the 1980s with companies like Dell, Tandem, and Compaq, a company founded in 1982 by three senior managers from Texas Instruments. Compaq was eventually sold to Hewlett-Packard for $25 billion in 2002.[11]

Texas continues to grow steadily as a global technology leader because of its probusiness stance. The state's tech industry has an annual economic impact—the dollar value of goods and services produced during a year—of $137 billion, according to 2017 data from the US Bureau of Economic Analysis.[12]

Texas ranks fourth in the nation for innovation, as measured by the number of tech startups and level of venture capital investments.[13] Texas currently ranks second in the nation by number of tech jobs, according to a 2018 report from the Computer Technology Industry Association, a global tech association that analyzed state-level workforce data.[14] Yes, our 963,000 tech jobs are still dwarfed by California, the number one state for tech employment with 1.7 million jobs.[15] But the gap is closing little by little as company after company relocates to greener pastures—in Texas.

Within the realm of "tech," there are several subcategories, and Texas maintains a strong, diversified presence in all of them, including computer systems and software development, online services, data centers, and video gaming.

Texas ranks number one nationally for cloud and data services jobs, according to the US Bureau of Labor Statistics.[16] The data services sector accounts for roughly 15 percent of the state's information technology services employment.[17] As of 2015, there were more than seven hundred cloud and data services companies here employing more than 30,500 workers.[18]

Folks, this growth didn't just magically happen. It took a proactive conservative stance to ignite growth. There's no inherent reason for the state to be a leader in data centers, other than the fact that the laws are more favorable here for their growth.

Throughout Texas's history, as new industries sprang forth with an economic benefit, our conservative leaders cleared a path for them to thrive—even if it meant reversing previously passed laws. In June

2011, the Texas Legislature passed Texas House Bill 1841, which gives tax advantages to data center companies. That's a great legislative example of conservative leaders thinking with a chamber-of-commerce mind-set.

In June 2013, the Texas Legislature passed Texas House Bill 1223, which provides a sales-and-use tax exemption on equipment purchases for data centers of at least one hundred thousand square feet that invest $200 million over five years and create at least twenty full-time permanent jobs paying 120 percent of a county's average weekly wage. With the law, data centers no longer have to pay sales tax every time they refresh equipment, which major data centers typically do every three or four years.

For the last five years, the Dallas area has ranked in the top three data center markets in the country—yes, outranking even Silicon Valley.[19] Northern Virginia is the nation's largest market, and Chicago and Dallas go back and forth as number two and number three, with Silicon Valley as a close number four, according to an April 2018 *Dallas Business Journal* article.[20]

Anthony Bolner, an executive vice president and partner with Stream Data Centers, said in the article that he doesn't see demand for data center space slowing anytime soon.

"The demand in our industry is really based on the growth of the Internet," he said. "It's things like autonomous cars and the Internet of Things. The demand for data center space right now is as strong as it's ever been, and it has grown exponentially over the last five to ten years."

Bolner's company is building 140,000 square feet of data center space on twenty-three acres east of Dallas. When completed, it will be their seventh data center in the Dallas–Fort Worth area. It's just one of several data center companies in Texas that were encouraged to set up shop because of the state's business-friendly tax policies.

Even the young millennials and Generation Xers that make up the lion's share of the industry know the value of a good ol' fashioned conservative tax savings. The 2018–2019 Texas budget sets aside $22 million for film and video game incentives.[21] Since 2009, when the state passed a digital production tax credit, employment in the video and online gaming industry jumped 49 percent, according to data from the Texas Economic Development & Tourism division.[22] Texas now ranks number two in the nation for entertainment software jobs.[23]

From the 2008–2009 biennium through 2015, the Texas Film Commission awarded more than $28.5 million in video game incentives to create forty-two hundred new jobs, according to the film commission's records.[24]

Texas Is an Energy Leader

But Texas leads in more than just the information sector. Oil discoveries may have put Texas on the map, but business-friendly tax policies and unobtrusive regulations fostered ingenuity to sustain it as an energy leader. Texas has a history of using its natural resources and conservative ideology to broker its own success.

Historians trace the state's oil discovery back to 1543, when survivors of the Hernando de Soto expedition used oil to caulk their boats after being forced ashore near the Sabine Pass.[25] Throughout the mid-1800s, Texans had minor oil discoveries while digging water wells, according to records from the Texas State Historical Association.[26] But on Friday, January 10, 1901, just outside of Beaumont, Texas, a hump of dirt known by the locals as Big Hill erupted with oil, changing the state's fate forever. History would refer to it as Spindletop.

According to Bryan Burrough's research in the book *The Big Rich: The Rise and Fall of the Greatest Texas Oil Fortunes*, Spindletop not only created the modern American oil industry but changed the way the world used oil.[27] So much black crude flowed from Beaumont that oil prices dropped to three cents a barrel—a cup of water cost five cents—making it economical for railroads and steamship companies to convert from coal to oil. The Santa Fe Railroad went from 1 oil-fired locomotive in 1901 to 227 in 1905, according to research in Daniel Yergin's book *The Prize: The Epic Quest for Oil, Money & Power*.[28] The rush to drill near Spindletop triggered the greatest speculative boom since the California Gold Rush.

Since that discovery, Texas's natural resources, skilled labor force, environmental research, and probusiness laws have made it an energy leader. The energy sector contributes more than $172 billion annually to the Texas economy, according to the Texas Economic Development Division.[29]

Texas is the only state in the contiguous United States with its own electric grid. Our electrical transmissions and new energy development are free from federal regulation. The history of our electrical independence dates back to the early 1900s, when small power plants started popping up across the state. These plants began linking together to provide electricity access to help support efforts in World War I and World War II. They also had another objective: staying out of reach of federal regulators.

In 1935, president Franklin D. Roosevelt signed the Federal Power Act, giving the Federal Power Commission the authority to regulate interstate electricity sales. Since Texas utilities never crossed state lines, they weren't subjected to federal rules. Today, there are three grids in the lower forty-eight states: the Eastern Interconnection, the Western Interconnection—and Texas.

Whether or not those who decry Texans as oil-drenched savages believe it, we also have the largest renewable energy production in the nation. There are more than forty-eight hundred companies employing more than 55,600 Texans in clean energy sectors, according to records from the Texas Economic Development Division.

Texas's Strong Military

Leading Texan technology and Texan energy, founded on firm conservative principles, have helped propel Texas to its current success, but one of the most important aspects of a constitutional conservative mentality is a strong national defense, and Texas has that as well. Texas is a strategic state, and not just in terms of military might, as seen at Fort Hood in Killeen and Fort Bliss in El Paso. Texas also has become a go-to source for the latest in disruptive defense technology, as seen with companies like Lockheed Martin and Raytheon in Fort Worth.[30]

During World War II, Texas became a critical state for military training because of its available land, number of bases, and general public support for the military.

San Antonio was home to the Third and Fourth armies, which oversaw basic and advanced training in several southern and western states. More than two hundred thousand airmen trained in Texas, which had more than fifty airfields and air stations, including naval air stations at Corpus Christi, Beeville, and Kingsville, according to records from the Texas State Historical Association.[31]

About 750,000 Texans (roughly 6 percent of the national total) saw military service during the war.[32] Texas claimed 155 generals and twelve admirals, including the supreme Allied commander in Europe, Dwight D. Eisenhower, and Pacific Fleet admiral Chester W. Nimitz. Col. Oveta Culp Hobby directed the Women's Army Corps; Walter Krueger commanded the United States Sixth Army.

The most decorated US soldier in World War II was Audie Murphy, born in Kingston, Hunt County, Texas. Murphy is an American military legend who exemplified the Texan spirit. His father deserted the family, and his mother died in 1941. To honor her life, Murphy enlisted in the army. Over the course of World War II, Murphy was awarded thirty-three US military medals, including three Purple Hearts and one Medal of Honor.

Texans move to the sound of guns. They are willing to be at the forefront, the tip of the spear when liberty is threatened.

The war had a tremendous impact on the Texas economy, in which federal and private investments brought massive industrial development. Aircraft production blossomed in Dallas–Fort Worth; shipbuilding boomed in Orange, Port Arthur, Beaumont, Houston, and Galveston. Sprawling industries along the Gulf Coast also formed the world's largest petrochemical center. Munitions plants, steel mills, and tin smelters were built, and increased demand for food, timber, and oil offered new opportunities throughout the state. With labor at a premium, half a million rural Texans moved to the cities.[33]

After the war, the United States kept a permanent military presence in Texas. Thousands of Texans served in the Korean conflict, in which native Texan Walton H. Walker held command of all United Nations ground forces from July to December 1950. During the 1960s and early 1970s, the nation's involvement in Vietnam dominated military affairs.

Texans and Texas-based forces also remained a major source of the nation's military strength through the 1980s and early 1990s. During the 1980s, Texas was second only to California for the most active-duty and retired military personnel.[34] Sprawling military complexes at San Antonio, El Paso, and Fort Hood, as well as defense manufacturing plants in the Dallas–Fort Worth area, had become essential to national defense as well as the state's economy.

When I was a young captain assigned to the First Infantry Division at Fort Riley, the strategic importance of Texas was very clear. As we prepped our vehicles and equipment for deployment to the Middle East for Operations Desert Shield and Storm in 1991, we loaded our gear up at the railhead to head to the port of Beaumont.

Today, Fort Hood and Fort Bliss are two major power projection bases for the United States Army. These installations are rivaled only by North Carolina and my birth state of Georgia. Later in my army career, I would be honored to command a field artillery battalion, Second Battalion, Twentieth Field Artillery, multiple launch rocket system in the Fourth Infantry Division, which at the time was stationed at Fort Hood, the world's largest military installation.

During my tenure as a battalion commander, we had an active component / reserve component agreement with the Texas Army National Guard. My third firing battery, Charlie Battery 2/20th FA, was actually part of the Texas National Guard. At the time, it was the only National Guard unit in the country equipped with the newest state-of-the-art rocket artillery system. Yes, the Texas National Guard.

During a National Training Center rotation supporting the Third Brigade of the Fourth Infantry Division, our division commander, MG Raymond T. Odierno, asked me if I was confident with Charlie Battery deploying with us to combat operations in Iraq. My answer was not just yes but, "Hell yes, sir, those fellas are raring to go. Give me two weeks of predeployment training, and they will be just as squared away as any active duty firing battery." See, Texans have and always will take to heart their responsibility to stand upon freedom's ramparts and be "Guardians of the Republic." Today, we need them to be Guardians of the Texas Republic.

You can't overstate the influence of the nation's military affairs on Texas history. The state's conservative values and respect for a strong national defense made it a safe place for training generations of men and women who fought faraway battles to protect freedoms at home. Our culture, society, economy, and demographic composition is largely influenced by the military.

Texan Success

While we'll discuss the low taxes, limited regulations, and attractive business incentives that have helped Texas succeed in further depth in Part Two of this book, for now, I want to offer you all some food for thought in the form of all the companies that are already thriving here and those itching to get here as fast as they can. In effect, Texas has been able to function like a well-oiled private equity fund, using California and other progressive socialist states as mere business incubators from which it can cherry-pick the most promising job creators.

Yes, the Dallas Cowboys, according to *Forbes* magazine, is the world's most valuable sports team at $4.2 billion, but I'll spare you the hoopla around "America's Team," as I'm still a devoted Atlanta Falcons fan.[35] Instead, I'll just stick to facts of a few industry-leading companies that relocated to Texas and now exemplify Texan values.

Exxon Mobil Corp.

Though we've already established Texas is much more than the oil companies that made it famous, and I have even more to say on that subject, it does seem fitting to start with ExxonMobil.

In the early years of Texas oil, one of the most profitable companies was Humble Oil & Refining, which was formed in 1911 in Humble, Texas, by local oilmen who discovered "Texas tea" at Spindletop. The men who started the company now have Houston-area streets and public schools named in their honor. One of the men, Ross Sterling, leveraged his oil-business acumen to become the thirty-first governor of Texas.

Those owners of Humble Oil later sold half of the company to Standard Oil of New Jersey in 1919. Just like the history of Alexander Graham Bell's AT&T, the federal government forced John D. Rockefeller's Standard Oil to breakup into thirty-three independent companies. Fast-forward past decades of legal battles and rebranding initiatives, and Standard Oil of New Jersey eventually becomes Exxon Corp., based in Manhattan.

In October 1989, Exxon announced it would be moving its headquarters from Manhattan to a 132-acre office park near Dallas. Exxon's chairman, Lawrence G. Rawl, said the company had concluded that "the Dallas area offered the best combination of factors from the standpoint of our employees' personal and professional lives and from an overall business standpoint," according to an October 27, 1989, article in the *New York Times*.[36]

It became an all-too-familiar narrative for Manhattan; two years earlier, J. C. Penney & Co. also left the city in a huff for the Dallas area, saying the move would save them $60 million a year in rent.[37]

What's entertainingly savage about the whole ordeal is that Exxon didn't even call city officials before announcing its decision to leave. Saving face, New York officials tried to downplay Exxon's decision. "This is an individual relocation," said Stanley Grayson, New York City's deputy mayor for finance and economic development. "It's part of an industry which I think is generally perceived as a southwest, Texas-based industry. It's part of an industry that's half the size it was ten years ago. Its outlook is not necessarily bright, and it's not perceived as a tremendous growth industry right now."[38]

"Not necessarily bright"? Hogwash! Since reconnecting with its Texas roots, Exxon has grown substantially, merged with Mobil, and now is a $237.2 billion company.[39] ExxonMobil is the world's most profitable company and is a beacon of Texan excellence.

Contrary to the New York officials erroneous forecast, the oil and gas industry is still poised for growth, and with ExxonMobil's legendary conservative business strategy, the company stands to be a profit generator for years and years to come.

ExxonMobil explores, produces, transports, and sells natural gas, crude oil, and related products globally. As of December 31, 2017, it had approximately 25,827 net operated wells with proved reserves of 21.2 billion oil-equivalent barrels.[40]

Our national exports of crude oil and liquefied natural gas continue to rise, which dovetails nicely with the new administration's goal of energy dominance for the United States. To be sure, the United States is still a major importer of crude oil, but we're growing as a low-cost supplier and exporter of energy. And that's good news for changing our position in the global energy landscape.

USAA

If you're looking for a company that honors Texan military culture, though, look no further than USAA—formally known as the United Services Automobile Association. The company exemplifies Texan success. The San Antonio-based provider of financial services and insurance serves customers with a military affiliation. It's fitting that the company is based in Texas, a state with a rich history of supporting the military.

The company has steadily grown in an extremely volatile industry because of conservative business principles. USAA reported $2.4 billion in net income, up 36 percent from 2016.[41] Instead of paying stockholders, USAA distributes its profits to its members.

They had a strong year even though 2017 presented a record catastrophe season in which USAA paid out more than $2 billion to thousands of members recovering from multiple natural disasters.[42] In addition, noncatastrophe losses increased as a result of normal growth in the number of auto policies, industry-wide trends in rising costs for auto parts and repairs, and an increase in the number of homeowner claims.

Even with these higher, uncontrollable losses, USAA operations remain solid, as reflected by increasing premium growth and healthy member retention.[43] The company's diverse business model—including banking, life insurance, and investment management operations—helped contribute positively to USAA's net income. The strong stock and commercial real-estate markets, along with improved bond yields—a result of higher interest rates—helped propel USAA's investment income to $3.2 billion.[44]

Thanks to USAA's conservative financial management, the company kept overall expense ratios low. Their property and casualty division achieved an operating expense ratio approximately 17 percent better than the industry.[45]

Texas laws paved the way for USAA to exist in its current form. Unlike most other Fortune 500 companies, USAA is not a corporation but rather an interinsurance exchange, thanks to the Texas Insurance Code. This insurance exchange is made up of current and former military officers and noncommissioned officers who have taken out property and casualty policies with USAA. Essentially, they are insured by each other. As a group, they own USAA's assets.

Normally, if there were a catastrophe threatening the financial health of the insurance exchange, each member would be held responsible for the losses. Err . . . that's also called socialism; that's not very Texan. However, the Texas Insurance Code added a provision (Section 942.152) that stipulates that an interinsurance exchange can limit member liability only to the premiums or premium deposits that the subscribers have paid to USAA.[46]

USAA was founded in 1922 in San Antonio when twenty-five army officers came together to insure each other's automobiles. Today, the company handles the affairs of nearly every person in the United States military across the world. I've been with USAA since I first joined the army in 1983. For me, their success is personal. In fact, their previous CEO, General Joe Robles, was one of my commanders when I was a young captain. I am proud to be personally insured by USAA and proud to see it based in Texas and benefitting from Texan success.

American Airlines

The world's largest airline is based in Fort Worth, Texas. To better understand how American Airlines has become the world's largest airline, it might help to look at the recent decision of an airline a fraction of its size.

In April 2018, the leaders at JetSuite Inc., a charter airline based in Santa Monica, California, announced plans to relocate the airline to Dallas.[47] JetSuite CEO Alex Wilcox said the decision to relocate was simple.

"I tried to start flying out of Santa Monica, California. And they sued me because I was trying to bring a service to the city," Wilcox said in an April 13, 2018, article in the *Dallas Business Journal*. "And when I got to Dallas, literally people in city hall were like, 'How can we help you?'

"It's such a welcome sea change," he added. "Not being viewed as an enemy but being viewed as an asset is so refreshing."[48]

JetSuite, which currently generates upward of $60 million in annual revenue, has now become one of thousands of middle-market companies finding success in Texas.[49]

American Airlines generated $42.2 billion in 2017 revenue.[50] For the airline company, Texas is a safe haven in an industry with unprecedented federal regulations and labor union exposure. Pilots, flight attendants, and mechanics all take turns dragging their airline employers to the negotiating table for more money and benefits. The last thing an airline needs is an adversarial relationship with the city, county, and state where it is trying to do business.

You'd be hard pressed to find an industry more regulated than the airlines. The Federal Aviation Administration's regulations and related fees for airlines are enough to make your head spin. Since 1960, 496 airlines have ceased operations.[51] Today, only a handful remain.

Before Fort Worth, American Airlines was headquartered at 633 Third Avenue in Midtown Manhattan, New York City. The company flew its headquarters—and thirteen hundred jobs—south to Texas in 1979.[52] In a tantrum, then New York City Mayor Ed Koch described the move as a "betrayal" of New York City, according to a November 16, 1978, article in the *New York Times*.[53] No, it wasn't a betrayal; it was excellent foresight for the future of the company.

American Airlines was created in 1930 from a merger of smaller airlines into a holding company, the Aviation Corporation, which was rebranded as American Airways and later as American Airlines in 1934.

The company has grown through strategic acquisitions, including Trans World Airlines in 2001 and US Airways in 2013.

Toyota of North America Inc.

Another transportation company has found success in Texas—on its roads instead of in its skies. Toyota Motor Corp. has been in the United States for sixty years and invested $22 billion over that period, according to the company's records.[54]

The company's April 2014 announcement to move its North American sales headquarters from California to Texas was met with widespread disbelief in Torrance, the city just outside of Los Angeles where Toyota had run its US operations since 1982.[55]

According to a report from Reuters, Torrance Mayor Frank Scotto looked grim standing outside of city hall Monday, April 28, saying he was blindsided by the move.[56] Days earlier, a Toyota official sent a message preparing Scotto to expect a call at 9:45 a.m. that Monday, just before the company would announce its decision to the world.

"At first I thought it was about something else," Scotto told Reuters on the day of the announcement. "Even this morning, despite all the rumors this weekend, we thought it was only going to be part of Toyota moving—not just everything." The decision, he said, was "sad news."

At the time, the two biggest employers in Torrance—which then had 147,000 people—were Toyota and Honda. Both employers had roughly four thousand employees. Losing Toyota meant losing an annual $1.2 million in tax revenue, Scotto said. The year before Toyota left, Torrance had an annual budget of $271 million and $121 million of long-term debt.

But when it comes to saving money, there's no love lost. Sentimentality takes a backseat. Proof? Scotto's son-in-law worked for Toyota, so the mayor faced the prospect of his daughter and grandchildren also moving to Texas.

During the press conference, the mayor conceded that the battle to keep Toyota was lost before it had even begun. "The train has already left the station," he said, adding that Torrance does not bear all the blame but that it takes the state of California to stop large manufacturers from leaving.

Frank Portillo, a co-owner of Los Chilaquiles Mexican Grill next to the old Toyota headquarters in Torrance, told Reuters at the time that he did not blame Toyota, although he might lose business himself. "The taxes are lower in Texas," Portillo said. "There are fewer regulations. It's cheaper for a company there. Why wouldn't they leave California?"

The main driver of Toyota's move from Torrance was housing costs, according to Albert Niemi Jr., dean of the Cox School of Business at Southern Methodist University, who has inside knowledge about the move.[57] The *Dallas Business Journal* reported on Niemi's assessment from an SMU Cox Economic Outlook Panel in December 2015.

"It wasn't so much that we don't tax income," he said. "It was really about affordable housing. That's what started the conversation. They had focus groups with their employees. Their people said, 'We're willing to move. We just want to live the American Dream.'"

Toyota did the math and found that housing costs in Los Angeles County, where Torrance is located, are three times per square foot the cost of a house in Dallas–Fort Worth.

"They're paying the same salary," Niemi said. "So in real terms, they're going to triple the affordability of housing they can buy if they move to Texas."

In North Texas, median home prices are three to four times the median income, said Chuck Dannis, real estate adjunct professor at SMU and senior managing director of National Valuation Consultants. In Torrance, homes cost about seven times the median income.[58]

The median home in Dallas–Fort Worth costs about $210,000, and the median income is roughly $58,000, Dannis said. In Torrance, the median home price is $508,000 and the median income is $76,000.

To be sure, Toyota has been careful to not blame California for its departure. Instead, the company diplomatically cites geography as a reason for leaving, as it's now closer to manufacturing plants in southern states.

"It may seem like a juicy story to have this confrontation between California and Texas, but that was not the case," Jim Lentz, Toyota's North American CEO, told the *Los Angeles Times* in a May 1, 2014 article. "It doesn't make sense to have oversight of manufacturing 2,000 miles away from where the cars were made. Geography is the reason not to have our headquarters in California."[59]

OK, Jim. But that also begs the question, why did Toyota decide to position its manufacturing plants in conservative states? I think you and I might see why.

In 2015, Toyota exported more than 160,000 US-built vehicles to forty countries, helping to establish the United States as a global export hub. Recent manufacturing expansions by Toyota in the United States include:

- $360 million investment in Toyota's Georgetown, Kentucky, plant, adding 750 new jobs.
- $150 million investment at its Huntsville, Alabama, plant.
- $100 million investment in Toyota's Princeton, Indiana, plant, adding 300 jobs.
- $90 million investment at its Buffalo, West Virginia, plant, adding 80 jobs.[60]

Do you honestly think it's a coincidence that all of those investments were in conservative states? If you do, bless your heart.

"Over the next five years, we're going to invest $10 billion in our plants to make them more competitive, in a new headquarters going into Texas, and into autonomous vehicles," Lentz said in a January 2017 article of the *Dallas Business Journal*.[61]

AT&T Inc.

Moving away from transportation back to technology, AT&T Inc.'s storied history is quintessential American business history, from a revolutionary telephone patent in 1876 to an antitrust case breaking up a monopoly in 1982. Since then, Texas has played the role of both operator connecting AT&T to growth and technician clearing channels for its profits. Today, AT&T pulls in more than $160 billion in annual revenue, ranking as the world's largest telecommunications company and the second-largest Texas-based company.[62]

Alexander Graham Bell created the Bell Telephone Company in 1879, which morphed into the American Telephone and Telegraph Company—AT&T Co.—in 1885. For the next one hundred years, New York City–based AT&T expanded its reach, bought competitors, and became essential to everyday life. Bell's patent expired in 1893, but his company still dominated by setting up twenty-two local telephone companies across the nation. That control alarmed federal regulators.

AT&T Co. reached an antitrust settlement with the government in January 1982, forcing it to break up into seven independent Regional Bell Operating Companies. The smallest of those seven companies was Southwestern Bell Corporation. Though it was the smallest and least likely to succeed among the seven, it had the advantage of Texas and an aggressive leadership.

In September 1992, Southwestern Bell announced it would leave its St. Louis, Missouri, headquarters for San Antonio, Texas. Southwestern Bell chairman Edward Whitacre Jr. cited customer expectations in the highly competitive telecommunications industry as a reason for the move to Texas.

"We're a service business," he said, according to a *United Press International* story during the time. "And service businesses succeed when they are close to their customers. This move will put us closer to more of our major growth markets and customers."[63]

Being close to Mexico also weighed in the decision, as the company was working through a deal with Telmex, the Mexican telephone company.

At the time, Southwestern Bell Corp. was a $9.3 billion company.[64] Texas governor Ann Richards said at a press conference in San Antonio that AT&T's decision gave Texas an "economic development gold medal."[65] But no one could predict then that the relationship would be as dynamic as it turned out to be.

Soon after its Texas relocation, Southwestern Bell Corp. changed its name to SBC Communications to position itself as a national telecommunications company. It started purchasing complimentary businesses nationwide, growing exponentially year after year.

On January 31, 2005, SBC announced it would purchase AT&T Corp. for more than $16 billion.[66] Stockholders and the Federal Communications Commission approved the merger later that year. SBC decided to take on the name of its predecessor, AT&T Inc.

The acquisitions kept coming, as did the revenue and profits. On May 18, 2014, AT&T announced it had agreed to purchase DirecTV, now known as AT&T Entertainment, for $48.5 billion.[67]

In June 2018, after six hundred days of effort, AT&T closed on the $85 billion purchase of the Time Warner media company, giving it some of the most respected names in Hollywood, including HBO,

Warner Bros., and Turner, along with new advertising opportunities.[68] The move came after a judge pushed back against the federal government's effort to block the deal on antitrust concerns.

Now the company is moving quickly to show what it can do with the high-profile asset as it rolls out new services, eyes more acquisitions, and invests in new content. In many ways, it's looking westward to take on younger rivals with names such as Amazon.com, Netflix, and Hulu. AT&T, while hardly the first to make a move on content, has bet big and has extensive plans.

Omnitracs

Omnitracs is a software firm that manages applications for the trucking industry. The company relocated its headquarters from San Diego to Dallas thanks in part to a $3.9 million check from the Texas government. In exchange for the $3.9 million, Omnitracs agreed to create 450 jobs and make a $10 million capital investment.[69]

Omnitracs CEO John Graham told the *San Diego Union-Tribune* in a July 18, 2014, article that he was excited about the move to Dallas.

"Establishing Dallas as our new headquarters will further solidify our industry leadership position, allowing us to centralize operations and better serve our growing multi-national customer base," Graham said. "As a major transportation hub with a technology-savvy workforce, we believe Dallas offers great advantages that align with our long-term business vision. Our new headquarters location places us closer to many of our fleet customers to ensure we can quickly and efficiently meet their evolving mobile technology needs."[70]

The company had three hundred employees based in San Diego.[71]

Omnitrac's history began thirty years ago when a startup called Qualcomm took an early computer-based tracking system and married it to a new communications network. They used this invention to help locate and message fleets of long-haul trucks. Qualcomm called this new mobile truck-tracking and communication system OmniTRACS.

Back in the late 1980s and much of the 1990s, San Diego–based Qualcomm grew much more famous for its development of cellphone, chipset, and processing technologies for the mobile communications networks on which the world now heavily depends. But OmniTRACS, which gradually morphed into the Omnitracs division of the company, was always at Qualcomm's core, quietly leading the digital revolution in trucking and logistics.

In 2013, Vista Equity Partners acquired the Omnitracs division of Qualcomm. The move to Texas, announced in July 2014, completed the exodus of three local companies owned by Vista Equity Partners.[72]

In all, Vista Equities, which has a history of moving companies out of California, received $17 million from the Texas Enterprise Fund to move the three companies out of San Diego.[73]

"Employers of all sizes and from all industries know that Texas's model of low taxes, smart regulations, fair courts and skilled workforce provide the best chance for their success now and well into the future," then Texas governor Rick Perry said at the time. "Omnitracs is the latest employer to call Dallas home, creating hundreds of jobs in the area and pumping millions in capital into the local economy."[74]

Fluor Corp.

Irving, Texas–based Fluor Corp. is one of the world's largest engineering and construction services companies, serving more than four thousand clients in more than one hundred countries.[75] To give you a sense of its size and capabilities, upon completion of major combat operations in Iraq, Fluor was awarded more than $1.1 billion in contracts to help rebuild water, power, and civic infrastructure.[76] The company had a 2017 revenue of $19.5 billion, up 7.7 percent from $18.1 billion in revenue in 2015.[77]

In May 2005, Fluor joined the corporate exodus from California to Texas. Their desire to relocate must have been strong, given how long they had been in California. John Simon Fluor started the company bearing his name in 1912 from a garage in Santa Ana, California. The company grew quickly, building oil refineries and pipelines in California and then globally.

Expansion grew tougher over the years because of their location. They wanted to move to Texas so bad that they didn't even demand relocation incentives or tax breaks to move here. About 80 percent of their domestic customer base was already in Texas or on the East Coast, and 60 percent of their contract backlog was with overseas clients that could be better served from a Texas location, according to a May 11, 2005, article in the *Los Angeles Times* announcing the move.

"We gain two hours with the time zone change and three hours in flight time" by moving, said then Fluor CEO Alan J. Boeckmann.[78]

Texas can't help the fact that it's centrally located for interstate travel. That's a trait, one of the many blessings we come by naturally. What we can take credit for is keeping a conservative, business-friendly, welcoming environment so companies like Fluor can flourish.

The nature of what Fluor does is to execute conservative values of staying on the client's budget. When your top repeat business for more than a century comes from some of the world's largest companies, municipalities, and governments, you must have built a reputation of doing stellar work while staying on budget.

Jacobs Engineering

Jacobs Engineering—which does work in everything from architecture to aerospace, mining, and transportation—announced in October 2016 it was moving its seventy-year-old headquarters from Pasadena, California, to Dallas.[79]

"As we continue to focus on transforming our business in terms of efficiency and high-growth in the engineering and construction industry, our new headquarter location ensures access to top talent and positions Jacobs for convenient access to our clients," Jacobs chairman and CEO Steven Demetriou said in a statement. "In Dallas, we will also benefit from a business-friendly economic and cultural environment."[80]

Jacobs received a Texas Enterprise Fund grant of $1.3 million to help pay for the move.[81]

Throughout the state of Texas, Jacobs employs nearly forty-five hundred employees working in the aerospace, transportation, water, aviation, buildings, defense, oil and gas, and power and energy industries.[82]

"Texas is already home to more than 50 Fortune 500 companies, and I am proud to announce today it will be home to one more," said Governor Abbott. "Because of our robust economic environment, more businesses are choosing to call Texas home. I would like to welcome Jacobs Engineering Group as the latest business to relocate its headquarters from California to the Lone Star State."[83]

Pasadena residents weren't completely surprised by Jacobs's move. For months, the city's officials had been meeting with Jacobs executives to encourage them to stay. At the time of its announcement, Jacobs already had been shifting jobs away from California. Of the company's sixty thousand employees, only two hundred were in Pasadena.[84] The editorial board of Jacobs's hometown newspaper, the *Pasadena Star-News*, summed up the departure this way:

"It's the end of an era for yet another California business. And the move inevitably raises comparisons with recent moves by other Southern California companies, including Toyota Motor Corp.'s North American division and coffee-maker Farmer Bros., which have also decamped for Texas.

"In many ways, Texas offers a better business climate than California, with fewer regulations, touted by its governor on trips to our state aimed at poaching employers. California politicians ignore the trend at their and our peril, and need to work harder to ensure we stay a business-friendly state."

Dean Foods Company

Dallas-based Dean Foods Co. is one of the world's largest dairy corporations. The company's roots trace back to 1925, when Samuel E. Dean purchased an evaporated milk processing facility in north-western Illinois. The company went public in 1961 as the Dean Milk Company; it changed to Dean Foods Company in 1963. The company continued to grow in the 1970s through 1990s.

I know what you're thinking: "Lt. Col. West, that has nothing to do with Texas!" Well, the story behind how Dean Foods became Texan highlights the conservative principles we've been talking about so far.

Dallas-based Suiza Foods Corp. purchased Dean Foods in 2001 and opted to keep the Dean Foods name. Simply put, the Texas economy that enabled Suiza to grow was far superior to the economy that put Dean Foods in a position to be acquired.

Suiza Foods had its start in 1988 when an investment firm led by Gregg Engles—a Dallas-based mergers and acquisition specialist—purchased the Reddy Ice packaged ice business for $26 million from the owners of Dallas-based 7-Eleven convenience store chain.[85] In late 1993, Engles and a group of partners acquired Suiza–Puerto Rico for $99.4 million.[86] That acquisition included Suiza Dairy Corp., one of the world's largest dairy companies. Engles saw an industry ripe for consolidation. His probusiness Texan spirit pushed him to acquire a string of dairy companies nationwide, including Dean Foods.

In Texas, the company has grown to roughly $7 billion in annual revenue, according to its publicly released financial records.[87] The company has stayed in front of consumer trends and buying habits with aggressive acquisitions and joint ventures.

Jamba Juice

Of all the many businesses we've looked at, however, Jamba Juice's decision to leave Emeryville, California, for Frisco, Texas, is probably the most comprehensive case study to show the philosophical and economic differences between the progressive socialist environment of California and the conservative environment of Texas.

"With the pending expiration of our lease in Emeryville at the end of 2016, we explored a number of location options that would offer us competitive operating costs, a region with extensive access to skilled restaurant talent, an attractive cost of living to our current and future team members and a geographical location that facilitates our ability to expand our store base," said David A. Pace, chief executive officer of Jamba, Inc. "The State of Texas meets all of these criteria and Frisco is a community committed to healthy living that aligns closely with our overall mission."[88]

Jamba's move to Frisco, Texas, is in line with population trends. Frisco is the nation's fastest-growing city, according to US Census Bureau data.[89] Though the North Texas city is still relatively small with 177,000 people, it is growing an average of 8.2 percent a year.[90] Frisco's economic development team aggressively advertises relocation incentives and site selection services prominently on its website. There's no secret to their intentions for growth.

In June 2018, the city received the highest municipal bond rating possible, translating into financial savings for the city in the form of lower interest rates.[91] Moody's Investors Service upgraded the city's bond rating to Aaa from Aa1, citing Frisco's "healthy revenue growth" and "strong fiscal position."[92] The Aa1 rating demonstrates the strongest creditworthiness relative to other US municipal or tax-exempt issuers or issues.

Moody's also recognized Frisco's proactive financial management practices to increase its operating expenditure reserves or "rainy day fund."

"Increasing reserves is a City Council priority," said Nell Lange, assistant city manager. "Our city policy sets the goal at 25 percent. We're proud to have ended the last fiscal year (FY17) with 43 percent in reserves. We couldn't do that without council leadership, specifically the Budget and Audit Committee."[93]

By comparison, Emeryville is in financial trouble. It's a small city of only 2.25 square miles, sandwiched between Berkeley and Oakland, extending to the shore of San Francisco Bay. It used to be a major industrial wasteland; however, in later years, the city reinvented itself to attract corporate headquarters for companies like Pixar, Peet's Coffee and Tea, and a host of biotech startups.

Other businesses and residents are soon likely to follow Jamba Juice's example because Emeryville is facing a $1.2 million shortfall this budget cycle and is on a trajectory to reach an estimated $6 million by 2020/2021.[94] Emeryville's municipal finance consultant, Susan Mayer, recently laid out the city's predicament and warned of impending costs and forces that could cause the gap to widen.

Mayer said that eroding revenues, cost pressures, and impending cost adjustments from the California Public Employees Retirement System are contributing to the gap. "Pension costs are the elephant in the room," Mayer warned city officials during a recent meeting, according to a report from *The E'ville Eye Community News.* "The increases are *truly* staggering."[95]

The California Public Employees Retirement System recently lowered its investment returns assumption and revealed that their pension plan is billions more in debt than previously forecast.[96] That debt means that cities like Emeryville, with just 11,671 residents, could be on the hook for millions in increased pension contributions. The city already issued a citywide hiring freeze.

During the meeting, Mayer cautioned the city on using onetime funds to fix ongoing structural deficits, and she scolded the city council for its use of city personnel and vendors. "It is not an unlimited pool," she said, according to the *E'ville Eye*. "There was not an ability to fund all the services that were requested. You have some programs that are over budget. You have some programs where the costs estimates are understated."[97]

The city has a history of questionable progressive socialist financial decisions. Just before Jamba Juice announced it was leaving, the city implemented the 2015 Living Wage Ordinance and a Fair Workweek Ordinance, both of which were expected to cost around a half million dollars to rollout and administer.[98]

Whenever there are problems, it's a familiar habit for progressive socialists to reach in their medicine cabinet for their favorite drug of taxes. Emeryville is considering a sales tax increase, higher than its current 9.25 percent. One councilmember suggested raising Emeryville's transit occupancy tax and utility user tax; others have proposed initiatives like a cannabis dispensary license and soda tax to raise money, according to the *E'ville Eye*.[99]

In June, Emeryville residents voted to approve "Measure C," a $50 million affordable housing bond.[100] It's a bold effort by one of the region's smallest cities to make an impact on the housing crisis. The bond amounts to $4,284 in borrowing per resident to pay for affordable housing projects and antidisplacement programs.

"No other jurisdiction in the East Bay has gone all out like this to raise money for affordable housing and anti-displacement programs," reads a report in a May 16, 2018, article in the *East Bay Express*.[101] Measure C bonds will be paid back over thirty years through a property tax of 4.9¢ per $100 of assessed value, meaning that the tax is relatively progressive and shouldn't be an undue burden on the average Emeryville resident.

In my opinion, however, Jamba Juice escaped a mess and landed in a growing city with strong conservative leadership.

The Migratory Pattern

Are you seeing a pattern in the successful businesses cited here? Many have left California, New York, or other "blue" states to find more success in Texas. Texan policies are providing a fertile ground for its economy and businesses to grow in. The data is telling. When one contrasts the thriving population, economy, and businesses of Texas against those in California, the differences become even more stark.

CHAPTER 4

THE DECLINE OF LIBERALISM

Why California Is Always a Seller's Market

Why are so many businesses leaving California for Texas? Unaffordable housing and high taxes, supported by progressive socialist policies, are working in tandem to lure Californians to other states. According to data from the American Community Survey, from 2007 to 2016 about 5 million people moved to California from other states, while about 6 million left California. On net, the state lost 1 million residents to domestic migration—about 2.5 percent of its total population.[1] California gained, on net, residents from about one-third of states, led by New York, Illinois, and New Jersey. On the flip side, top destinations for those leaving California were Texas, Arizona, Nevada, and Oregon, according to data from California's Legislative Analyst's Office.[2]

Unaffordable Housing

California has the highest median home values in the nation among the top twenty-five most populous states.[3] In 2017, the average Southern California home sold for $520,000. That's almost triple the median price of a US home, which sits at $188,900 according to the National Association of Realtors.[4]

California home prices and rents have increased faster than the national average since the 1940s, when the average California home cost about 20 percent more than the average US home.[5] But by the end of the 1940s, the state's home prices were 30 percent higher than average, according to the state's records.[6]

By 1970, home prices began to accelerate even more. By 1980, prices were 80 percent above US levels. By 2010, the typical California home was twice as expensive as the typical US home.

While much of California enjoys excellent weather, and while it is the center of one of the biggest industries in the nation, these factors alone don't account for housing costs. One reason for the high costs is California isn't building enough houses along the coastal areas. Two-thirds of Californians live in the state's major coastal metros—Los Angeles, Oakland, San Diego, San Francisco, San Jose, and Santa Ana–Anaheim, according to research from Mac Taylor of the Legislative Analyst's Office, the California legislature's nonpartisan fiscal and policy advisor.[7] When there's a shortage of houses, families are competing with each other for the best place to sleep. That competition jacks up prices.

In most areas, housing developers respond to excess demand by building more housing. However, in California's coastal metros, building permits issued by local officials remained flat. Between 1980 and 2010, construction of new housing units in California's coastal metros was low by national and historical standards, according to Taylor's research. During this thirty-year period, the number of housing units in the typical US metro grew by 54 percent, compared with 32 percent for the state's coastal metros.

Home building was actually slower in Los Angeles and San Francisco, where the housing stock grew by only 20 percent.[8] California's inland metros added housing at about twice the rate of the typical US metro between 1980 and 2010.[9] Yet housing costs in much of inland California are still above average relative to the rest of the country.[10] High housing costs in the state's inland metros appear to result largely from their proximity to California's coast. Some households and businesses that want to locate on California's coast but find housing too expensive there locate in California's inland metros instead. This displaced demand places pressure on inland housing markets and results in higher home prices and rents there, according to the state's Legislative Analyst's Office.

Although high land costs can translate into higher home prices and rents, it is possible to offset the effects of high land costs through more dense development. (The density of housing refers to the number of housing units per unit of land—typically measured in units per acre. Higher density housing, such as an apartment building, has more housing units per acre.) Building more units on the same plot of land allows a developer to spread land costs across more units, lessening the impact of land costs on the cost of each unit. This is because land costs are fixed and do not increase if a developer builds additional units.

For example, if a developer builds five homes on a plot of land that costs $100,000, the land cost per unit is $20,000. And if the developer builds ten homes on the same plot of land, the land cost per unit is only $10,000. Builders faced with high land costs, therefore, generally will build more dense housing. When this occurs, the effect of high land costs on home prices and rents is reduced. But in California, there's little increase in housing density in the coastal metro areas. The high land costs translate directly into higher housing costs.

Aside from the cost of land, a developer has three other major costs to consider when building: labor, materials, and government fees. All three are much higher in California than the rest of the country. Construction labor is about 20 percent more expensive in California metros than in the rest of the country, according to the state's Legislative Analyst's Office.[11] California's building codes and standards also are considered more comprehensive and prescriptive, often requiring more expensive materials and labor.

Although conditions in California—located on a fault line as it is—may require more comprehensive building codes for earthquake safety, Taylor's report hints there may be more to building costs in California than a requirement to make buildings safer for earthquakes. "The state requires builders to use higher quality building materials—such as windows, insulation, and heating and cooling systems—to achieve certain energy efficiency goals," Taylor said in his Legislative Analyst's Office report. "Additionally, development fees—charges levied on builders as a condition of development—are higher in California than the rest of the country."

A 2012 national survey found that the average development fee levied by Californian local governments—aside from water-related fees—was slightly more than $22,000 per single-family home, compared with about $6,000 per single-family home in the rest of the country.[12] Altogether, the cost of building a typical single-family home in California's metros is likely between $50,000 and $75,000 higher than in the rest of the country, according to data from California's Legislative Analyst's Office.[13]

So, clearly, higher building costs contribute to higher housing costs throughout the state. But when you look deeper, you'll find that the relationship between building costs and prices and rents differs across inland and coastal areas of the state. In the state's Legislative Analyst's Office report, it found that in places where housing is relatively abundant, such as much of inland California, building costs generally determine housing costs. This is because landlords and home sellers compete for tenants and homebuyers. The competition benefits renters and prospective homebuyers by depressing prices and rents, keeping them close to building costs. To me, that sounds like Texas; that's a good conservative principle at play. In these types of housing markets, building costs account for the vast majority of home prices. In two major inland metros—Riverside–San Bernardino and Sacramento—building costs account for more than four-fifths of home prices.[14]

In contrast, the Legislative Analyst's Office report found that in coastal California, the opposite is true. Renters and homebuyers compete for a limited number of apartments and homes, bidding up prices far in excess of building costs. Building costs account for around one-third of home prices in California's coastal metros. In these areas, increased competition for limited housing is the primary driver of housing cost growth.[15]

I know I'm not the sharpest knife in the drawer, but it seems clear to me that Californians could fix their housing crisis by simply building more houses. If people want to live along the coast, and there's open land, why not just build more housing to help drive down prices? Unfortunately, it appears there are a few concrete barriers to common sense.

For starters, there's widespread community resistance to new housing. Local communities make most decisions about housing development. When residents are concerned about new housing, they can use the community's land use authority to slow or stop housing from being built or require it to be built at lower densities. On the surface, that sounds fair to me. Lt. Col. West is all about giving power to the people.

But let's look closer at *why* there's resistance to new construction. The answer may rest in a forty-year-old law that has set up the state for failure.

On June 6, 1978, California voters passed Proposition 13, which immediately reduced property tax rates on homes, businesses, and farms by roughly 57 percent.[16] If you're a Texas resident, you're probably thinking, "We should try something like that." Well, hold your horses, partner! I agree that Texas property taxes are high, but this isn't the way to fix them.

Before Proposition 13, life was a little like Texas: property taxes were based on the market value of property—that is, the price for which it could be sold.

Under Proposition 13, property taxes instead are based on a property's purchase price. In the year a property is purchased, it is taxed at its purchase price. Each year thereafter, the property's taxable value increases by 2 percent or by the rate of inflation, whichever is lower. This process continues until the property is sold and again is taxed at its purchase price, according to a report from California's Legislative Analyst's Office.[17]

Prior to Proposition 13, if homes in a neighborhood sold for higher prices, neighboring properties might have been reassessed based on the newly increased area values. Under Proposition 13, the property is assessed for tax purposes only when it changes ownership. As long as the property is not sold, future increases in assessed value are limited to an annual inflation factor of no more than 2 percent.

Among the many problems a tax law like this creates is an overwhelming advantage to Californians who bought their homes a long time ago. It essentially created a mammoth rent-control subsidy for Californians who owned homes before 1978. In California, it makes more financial sense to stay put than it does to purchase a new home.

"It's one reason why the proportion of the state's properties that change hands each year fell from 16 percent in 1977 to less than 6 in 2014," writes Henry Grabar for *Slate* magazine's Moneybox blog.[18] That's why it's always a seller's market in California.

It's also why many longtime California homeowners are opposed to new housing construction. Those 1978 voters effectively snatched the dream of homeownership away from their kids. Building fewer houses than people demand drives up prices. That's just basic economics.

The law also promotes land hoarding. In California, it's extremely cheap to keep long-held land vacant, even if it has become extremely valuable. In Texas, however, you're more likely to sell vacant land, if for no other reason than to avoid paying escalating taxes on something you're not using.

Without a doubt, California has lost billions upon billions of dollars in lost property tax revenue. And unfortunately for Californians, cities now use a host of fees on new development—like impact fees, parcel taxes, and special assessments—to compensate for forgone property tax revenue. These produce tens of thousands of dollars in new revenue per building permit, a cost that gets passed on to new buyers, according to a September 22, 2016, article in *Slate* magazine.[19]

California also doesn't build more houses because its environmental reviews can be used to stop or limit housing development. Folks, this is progressive socialism at work. The California Environmental Quality Act (CEQA) requires local governments to conduct a detailed review of the potential environmental effects of new housing construction prior to approving it.[20] The findings can result in the city or county denying new housing proposals or approving fewer housing units than the developer proposed.

Surprise, surprise: there's now a problem in California with people abusing CEQA to file frivolous lawsuits to block infill housing. A January 2018 white paper published by the *Hastings Environmental Law Journal* found that the most frequent targets of CEQA lawsuits typically are required to undergo a rigorous environmental analysis and public review process that takes eighteen to thirty-six months or longer.[21] This process involves an environmental impact report and at least three rounds of public notice and comment before being eligible for approval by public votes of elected officials. Friends, that's the definition of "red tape."

"We found that too often enforcement of CEQA is aimed at promoting the economic agendas of competitors and labor union leaders, or the discriminatory 'Not In My Backyard' agendas of those seeking to exclude housing, park, and school projects that would diversify communities by serving members of other races and economic classes," writes Jennifer Hernandez, an environmental and land use lawyer for Holland & Knight and author of the white paper. "Anonymous CEQA lawsuits by parties seeking to conceal their identity and their economic interests in the outcome of lawsuits must end. CEQA's purpose is to protect the environment and human health, not advance economic agendas."

CEQA is one of the well-recognized culprits in California's housing supply and affordability crisis.

UC Berkeley economics professor Enrico Moretti, an advocate for increasing density and productivity in urban regions, wrote in a September 6, 2017, edition of the *New York Times* that CEQA's main effect today is making urban housing more expensive.[22] It has added millions of dollars of extra costs to a sorely needed high-rise on an empty parking lot on Market Street in downtown San Francisco.

The Bay Area's hills, beaches, and parks are part of the area's attractions, but there is enough underused land within its urban core that the number of housing units could be greatly increased without any harm to those natural amenities.

All of these barriers have created a major disconnect between the demand for housing and its supply. And there are no legitimate signs of change, even as droves of companies flee. The many state and local policies that have slowed or stopped development in recent decades are still in effect today. As a result, California's trend of rapidly rising housing costs is quite likely to continue in the future.

High Taxes

While unnecessary regulation and red tape make it difficult to obtain new land and build new places of business in California for many young companies—and hard for their Joe and Jane Six-Packs, working at those companies just to earn their living, to own a home or pay rent and maintain a decent quality of life—high taxes are also driving them away. At 13.3 percent, California has the nation's highest individual income tax rate. You could argue that legislators backed themselves into a corner by implementing Proposition 13 in 1978. It not only took potential property tax revenue off the table but created a wider wealth gap and made housing unaffordable for the middle class.

California began to depend heavily on personal income tax and sales tax for state revenue. Since the state could no longer depend on a growing property tax revenue, it became disproportionately reliant on these two taxes. During good times, when everyone is feasting, the state increases tax credits and exemptions. During times of famine, legislators increase tax rates and fees and find creative ways to negotiate an ongoing structural deficit.

Since 1979, there has not been a major reform of California's tax system, despite a widely acknowledged need for a major overhaul to address the state's bust and boom cycles.

Now add to the equation a historic technology boom—which they helped create. Today, the coastal region of the state is chockful of millionaire tech workers. Housing developers, naturally, are going to design living options and set prices to match those fabulous tech salaries. They'd be silly not to do so. But that adds to the wealth gap.

Now city, county, and California state officials are trying to tax their way back to solvency. And these billion-dollar tech companies have become the perfect piñata to beat for cash.

The $3 trillion neighborhood known as Silicon Valley wasn't built overnight. Reporters from Business Insider compiled a tech timeline in a May 20, 2017, blog post to give readers a sense of the rich history.[23] They traced the region's tech lore back to the late 1800s, when San Francisco's port helped make it a hub for the telegraph and radio industries.

As with many discoveries, the military also played a vital role in the region's tech reputation. The navy purchased Moffett Field in

1933 to dock and maintain the *USS Macon*. As a result, Moffett Field became a major hub for the early aerospace industry. Scientists and researchers began flocking to the area. In 1939, William Hewlett and Dave Packard founded Hewlett-Packard in Palo Alto to make oscilloscopes and, later, radar and artillery technology during World War II. Semiconductors were invented, implemented, and modified during the 1960s. By 1969, the Stanford Research Institute became one of the four nodes of ARPANET, a government research project that became a precursor to the internet. In 1970, Xerox invented early computing tech in Palo Alto. In 1971, journalist Don Hoefler titled a three-part report on the semiconductor industry "Silicon Valley USA." The name stuck.

In the 1970s, companies like Atari, Apple, and Oracle were all founded in the area. In the 1980s, Silicon Valley became the widely accepted center of the computer industry. eBay, Yahoo, PayPal, and Google are just some of the companies founded in the area in the 1990s. Facebook, Twitter, Uber, and Tesla followed them a decade later.

Through the years, especially during the dot-com boom era of the early 2000s, the region courted technology discovery, groomed entrepreneurs, and fostered their growth. It worked, arguably too well. City officials where these companies are headquartered mistakenly believed these tech millionaires and billionaires shared their same brand of progressive socialism. They probably thought, "Of course they'll be eager to voluntarily spread their wealth and fix our homeless situation."

But these companies have accumulated formidable power, and it would be a mistake to assign them to any one political party, writes

Noam Cohen in his book *The Know-It-Alls*. "The Know-It-Alls" represent "a merger of a hacker's radical individualism and an entrepreneur's greed," Cohen writes. They tend to "travel in Democratic Party circles but oppose unions, hate-speech codes, or expanded income redistribution."[24]

But now city officials are reaping the problems of their policies. Those very tech companies that they once boasted about are now more prosperous than the cities in which they're headquartered.

Google, for instance, now has enough money to essentially purchase a city for its workers and operations.[25] In June 2017, the San Jose City Council agreed to negotiate a major land deal with the online search engine company. Google had been making major development moves in downtown San Jose for years, before the city council finally negotiated a sale of sixteen parcels of land. Though the deal was supported by the mayor and vice mayor, the city's residents were a bit more hesitant, according to a June 21, 2017, article on Engadget.com.

Google's plan is to transform the Diridon Station area of San Jose into a massive transit hub. It is expected to be a Google village, adding upward of twenty thousand jobs. If given full approval, Google would build between 6 to 8 million square feet of office space and up to three thousand units of housing. However, San Jose residents are concerned it will displace them. They've urged the city council and mayor to make sure the project comes with necessary safeguards to keep housing affordable.

The success of Google and its peers, juxtaposed with the struggle of non-tech-working residents to keep up, has put pressure on local elected officials to do something—even as they simultaneously strike land deals to appease the companies.

Now throw in the Republican tax bill. Among many things, the Tax Cuts and Jobs Act of 2017 provides a historic tax cut for corporations. The federal tax rate falls from 35 percent to 21 percent, the largest one-time rate cut in US history for the nation's largest companies.[26] Overall, it amounts to roughly $1 trillion in tax cuts for businesses over the next decade.

With tech companies now saving billions on taxes, the progressive socialist city leaders where their companies are headquartered are chomping at the bit to cash in.

Not that this attitude is exclusive to California. In May 2018, Amazon.com Inc. threatened to move jobs out of Seattle, its hometown, in protest of a new tax on the city's top-grossing businesses. The online retailer told builders to stop construction on an office tower in down-town Seattle after the city council voted to approve an unfair tax.[27]

Seattle businesses with more than $20 million in annual revenue are charged twenty-six cents per employee for every hour worked, according to a report from the Seattle Business Journal.[28] The city esti-mates the tax will generate roughly $75 million per year for affordable housing and homeless services. Amazon is now on the hook for about $20 million annually.

Amazon had already been open about its search for a second head-quarters that would bring fifty thousand jobs and a capital investment of $5 billion. On its short list of twenty cities, Amazon included both Austin and the Dallas–Fort Worth area as possible landing spots.[29] Now that Seattle has moved forward with its tax, it could end up losing Amazon completely. Their loss might be our gain.

Yet California cities are still considering similar taxes on their largest employers to solve their solvency problems. The cities of San

Francisco, Mountain View, Cupertino, and East Palo Alto are all considering taxes to offset their respective deficits.

"Google has billions of dollars in cash floating around," said Lenny Siegel in a May 23, 2018, article published in the *Seattle Times*.[30] Siegel is the mayor of Mountain View, California, where Google is headquartered. "They made billions off the tax bill. They can afford to spend a little more here."

To his credit, Siegel didn't even waste time trying to be politically coy about why they're proposing a head tax. But what Siegel and his neighboring city officials fail to understand is that people often will sing loud and proud in the United Progressive Socialist Chorus . . . until you change the hymnal to "Wealth Redistribution." For business owners, that song is always out of tune.

Mountain View's proposed head tax on Google could cost the company $5.8 million per year for its twenty-four thousand employees based in the city. It's likely to pass, if Seattle's unanimous tax decision against Amazon is any indication.

We're now at a critical inflection point in the relationship between California's companies and its local governments. For years, tech companies have been able to sidestep problems by killing local taxes with "a mix of public posturing and backroom wrangling," according to the May 23, 2018, *Seattle Times* article. They used to satisfy their corporate social responsibility with simple neighborly gestures: Google funded an electric shuttle service in Mountain View; Amazon gave away bananas. That's no longer going to cut it. City officials want more.

In Amazon's case, Seattle initially proposed a tax of $500 per employee to put a temporary bandage on its homeless problem. Amazon flexed. Seattle relented. Amazon threatened to stop plans for a new office tower, so the city altered plans and cut the tax to $275 per employee for a total of about $50 million. Amazon has said it will continue with its building plans, but it remains "very apprehensive" about its future in the city.

How much leverage do cities have in pushing their corporate celebrities to pay more taxes? We're about to find out. The list of companies—tech and nontech—that have left California is growing with each passing financial quarter.

An attempt by California politicians to raise the state's corporate income tax rate will drive more businesses from the Golden State to Dallas–Fort Worth and other locales with similarly business-friendly laws and policies, a top site selection consultant and researcher predicts.

"I've got to tell you this has just caused an uproar out here," Joseph Vranich, president of Irvine, California–based Spectrum Location Solutions, told the *Dallas Business Journal* in a March 20, 2018, article. "If anything is representative of cruel and oppressive treatment, this has reached new levels."

Vranich was referring to an attempt led by Democratic State Assembly members in California to raise the state's business taxes in response to President Trump's federal tax overhaul.

The measure would more than double the state's corporate income tax rate, giving California the nation's highest rate of 18.84 percent, up from the current rate of 8.84 percent, the *Dallas Business Journal* reported. The legislators who sponsored the California amendment characterized it as "middle class tax justice" and argued that, given federal cuts in the corporate tax rates, businesses could afford to pay more in California taxes.

The proposed California rate would be three times the current median rate nationwide. It would raise corporate taxes on California companies with revenues higher than $1 million. The state tax hike would be for an amount equivalent to half what they received from the federal tax cut.

In November 2015, Vranich released research indicating that roughly nine thousand California companies had moved their headquarters or diverted projects to out-of-state locations in the prior seven years, and most of those had gone to Texas.[31]

Vranich said he hasn't updated the number of California move-outs since the 2015 report, but he senses growing dissatisfaction in the phone calls he gets from companies considering a move.

"I can't tell you that there has been an explosion of companies leaving California, but there is some evidence that the interest is intensifying," he told the *Dallas Business Journal* in an interview. "This is not the only tax increase being proposed on California businesses."

Some of the companies in Vranich's study relocated their headquarters, while others kept their headquarters in California but targeted out-of-state locations for expansions. The report did not count instances of companies opening a new out-of-state facility to tap a growing market—an act unrelated to California's business environment.

Learning from California

Now, I think California is a fantastic state. I am not trying to rag on California. After all, I did marry my love, Angela, there on Christmas Eve 1989 in the Big Bear Lake area. And I have memories—though not necessarily fond ones—of those training rotations to the National Training Center in the Mojave Desert.

California's contributions to our great nation cannot be overstated, but they've clearly got a problem. The Golden State is bleeding business—often to Texas. High property values due to overregulation and bureaucratic red tape make it unaffordable to own land and construct buildings. Taxes founded on an ideal of wealth redistribution make it unprofitable and unrewarding to be an entrepreneur. Companies are fighting back, and citizens are moving on to greener pastures.

I've spent some time pointing out the differences between Texas and California because the same ideological battle that has California businesses lining up to head to Texas is moving on over here. But the progressive socialist policies in California have created problems—problems we have to avoid in Texas.

PART TWO

NO SURRENDER

CHAPTER 5

THE FRIENDLY STATE

A Tax Code That Pays

Texas's conservative principles have stood the test of time, building an economy that means the state is growing exponentially. Texas is often known as the Friendly State: friendly for families, friendly for business, and friendly for the nation. I aim to keep it that way. Progressive socialists want to turn this great state blue, but I'm drawing the line in the sand. The conservative principles that have helped us succeed are worth fighting for.

One of the most important foundations for an economy and an environment that is favorable for businesses and individuals is a simple, favorable tax code.

In 2018, Americans will pay $3.4 trillion in federal taxes and $1.8 trillion in state and local taxes, for a total tax bill of $5.2 trillion, or 30 percent of national income.[1] That's more than the country was expected to spend on food, clothing, and housing, according to data from the US Bureau of Economic Analysis and calculations from the Tax Foundation.[2]

Clearly, the nation has a tax problem. It's the progressive socialists' addictive drug in their medicine cabinet of quick fixes.

Meanwhile, a healthier, more favorable tax code is luring people to Texas.[3] Our tax code, like that of all other states, is a varied system with several moving cogs and gears. It can be confusing at first glance, but if I can figure it out, you can too. It's important to grasp the basics to better understand what makes Texas so darn competitive for corporate relocations.

Let's take a look at four broad categories in Texas's tax code—individual taxes, corporate taxes, sales taxes, and property taxes.

Taxes on Workers

For starters, Texas doesn't have an individual income tax. Workers get to keep more of their paychecks here. That's not the case for forty-three other states, which rely on individual income taxes for a chunk of their state government revenue. Two of those states—Tennessee and New Hampshire—only tax dividend and interest income.

States get creative, arguably too creative, with their income tax requirements. Eight of the states with income taxes have single-rate tax structures, with one rate applying to all taxable income. However, thirty-three of those states instituted a graduated-rate income tax, which groups taxpayers in brackets based on their income. And the income bracket parameters vary widely among the states. Hawaii—birthplace of Barack Obama—actually leads the nation with twelve tax brackets. That's stressful, despite their beaches, luaus, and Polynesian dancers.

Hawaii's top marginal individual income tax rate is eleven percent. And that's not the nation's highest. California leads the nation with a 13.3 percent individual income tax rate, which explains why workers are eager to relocate to Texas—not to mention their employers, who have their own set of incentives to leave the Golden State.

For the married, some states double their single-bracket income tax parameters to keep from penalizing marriage. Some states make income tax bracket accommodations for inflation. And some link their standard deductions and personal exemptions to the federal tax code, while others set their own or none at all.

Did I mention that Texas doesn't have an individual income tax? It's just one of the little ways Texas tells its citizens they're welcome to live and work in our state.

Taxes on Companies

In addition, Texas also doesn't have a corporate income tax. Corporate income taxes are collected in forty-four states, but they typically account for only 5 percent of state tax collections and contribute less than 3 percent to a state's general revenue. So, it begs the question, why collect them?

According to the Tax Foundation, Iowa levies the highest top statutory corporate tax rate at 12 percent, closely followed by Pennsylvania at 9.99 percent and Minnesota at 9.8 percent. Three other states—Alaska, Illinois, and New Jersey—levy rates of 9 percent or higher.[4]

North Carolina's flat rate of 3 percent is the lowest rate in the country among states that collect corporate taxes, followed by rates in North Dakota (4.31 percent) and Colorado (4.63 percent).

To be sure, instead of a corporate income tax, Texas imposes a franchise tax on businesses. It is based on the company's margin, which Texas defines as the total revenue minus one of four possible deductions. It's complicated and controversial in Texas, especially as the state fights to keep its business-friendly street cred.

Yet the fact that Texas lawmakers ferociously debate the existence of this tax is a good sign for businesses. True conservative lawmakers are always wrestling and wrangling in the best interest of businesses, even when there's no simple answer for how to meet budget demands. As a business leader, that's what you want—lawmakers who position themselves as partners helping you succeed.

Taxes on Sales

For the most part, Texas is middle of the road on sales taxes. At 8.17 percent, the state's sales tax rate ranks twelfth in the nation.[5] Most people can understand sales taxes pretty easily. They're more transparent. In Texas, we're honest folk, for the most part. We like people to see their taxes.

What sets us apart is our gas tax. Generally speaking, conservative states have a lower gas tax than liberal leaning states. At twenty cents per gallon, Texas's gas tax is among the lowest in the nation. Pennsylvania, at fifty-eight cents per gallon, has the highest gas tax, followed by Washington, Hawaii, and New York.[6]

States typically use gas taxes for services that directly benefit drivers, such as highway construction, maintenance, and road repairs. But the percentage of gas tax revenue going toward those expenditures is declining over time. In many states—including Texas—gas tax revenue is not adjusted for inflation, so states have to look elsewhere to pay for road construction, repairs, and maintenance. Gas tax revenue to the Texas Department of Transportation hasn't seen an increase since 1991.[7]

It's in dilemmas like this that conservative principles go toe to toe with liberal principles. Some states, feeding their addiction, reach in the medicine cabinet and raise more taxes. Others, like Texas, work to avoid raising taxes for transportation expenses.

Taxes on Property

The state's Achilles heel is the property tax rate, which currently is among the nation's highest.[8] In short, property taxes here are so high because the state works to keep taxes low in other areas.

Our state law allows local governments to collect and use property taxes to fund roads, hospitals, emergency services, and schools. Reducing the tax is a perennial goal whenever state legislators come together, but it's important to remember that property taxes are just one piece of the equation. When you compare the overall tax burden with other states, Texas remains one of the lowest in the nation. And that's just one of many reasons why businesses are flocking here.

Why We're Keeping Taxes Low in Texas

Keeping taxes low and easy to understand encourages financial success. It promotes pursuing the American Dream and helps individuals work to secure their own rights and happiness better than any government could. But progressive socialists claim the government can do a better job of providing collective prosperity—just as long as citizens will give up some of their own.

We've talked about the problems of California's income tax and how Texas has benefited from not having one, but at the federal level, we still have a progressive tax system. As your income climbs the ladder, you are taxed higher. There have been a few favorable changes recently, but broadly speaking, it's still very much the same principle, and it causes problems, even in Texas.

Progressive socialists will continue to push for more taxes to fund their ideology of equality of outcomes. You can't do that and still say you're all for helping citizens achieve the American Dream. Somebody has to call out the hypocrisy.

Let me share a few specific, common-sense problems I have with the progressive income tax:

1. It's Unfair

The federal progressive income tax penalizes marriage. Are we really at the point now in our society where being married is a crime? It makes absolutely no sense for married people to be paying higher rates than singles living together. It's one of the unintended features of the United States' income tax system. The combined tax liability of a married couple may be higher than their combined tax burden if they had remained single.

Hmm, I'm pretty sure that's *not* what the Apostle Paul had in mind when he said in 1 Corinthians 7:7-8,

> I wish that all men were as I am. But each man has his own gift from God; one has this gift, another has that. Now to the unmarried and widows I say this: It is good for them to remain unmarried, as I am.

The marriage tax penalties typically occur when two individuals with equal incomes marry, regardless if you're rich or too po' to pay attention. An unmarried couple with equal incomes that earns a combined $300,000 would have a total tax bill of $83,232.50 ($64,374.50 from the individual income tax and an additional $18,858 from the payroll tax).[9] If they got married, they would be hit by a marriage penalty of $3,806.50. I could go into details explaining the math of how that happens, but both of us would fall asleep before I finished.

Now for those poor married couples—probably living off of love and a microwave in a one-bedroom apartment—the earned income tax credit has a significant impact on marriage penalties. Adding one partner's income to the other partner's income can easily push the combined income of the couple into the phaseout range of the earned income tax credit, according to the Tax Foundation.[10]

For a couple with equal incomes of just $15,000—$30,000 combined—with one child, their tax bill would be $1,594 due to the refundability of the $1,000 child tax credit and the $3,359 earned income tax credit received by the individual who claimed the child. If they were to marry, their combined tax bill would still be negative, but they would face a marriage penalty of $1,087.88.

It's possible to eliminate the marriage penalty to make the tax code more neutral with respect to marriage, but it would take a significant change to the income tax code.

Texas avoids all these problems by *not having an income tax*. The federal government could learn a thing or two from Texas.

2. It Costs Too Much

The hidden costs of tax compliance—the time and money spent on tax compliance, coupled with the opportunity cost of forgone economic growth—can cost up to $987 billion, according to a study published by the Mercatus Center at George Mason University.[11]

Part of the excessive cost is attributed to lawmakers using the tax code for purposes extending beyond simply collecting revenue to fund the federal government. Many lawmakers use special provisions inserted in the code to advance objectives ranging from increasing "fairness" to granting competitive advantage to favored businesses or industries, the study found.

In addition, Americans spend upward of $378 billion annually in accounting costs related to filing taxes, according to the study.

The average fee charged to prepare an itemized Form 1040 with Schedule A and a state tax return is $273, and the cost for a Form 1040 without itemized deductions and a state return is $176, according to a survey from the National Society of Accountants.[12] The data was reported in an article from CPA Practice Advisor.

Nearly half (49.8 percent) of tax and accounting practices increase tax-preparation fees annually, while 33.7 percent increase these fees every other year.[13] For accounting fees, 37.4 percent increase fees annually, while 34.4 percent increase fees every other year.

Surveyed firms expected to increase their accounting service fees by an average of 6.1 percent in 2017, up from an actual increase of 5.3 percent in 2016.[14]

Tax-preparation fees are expected to rise by higher percentages. Surveyed firms expected to increase tax-prep fees by an average of 6.4 percent in 2017, up from an actual increase of 6.0 percent in 2016.[15]

Nearly three-quarters (71 percent) charge an added fee for disorganized or incomplete files. Another 33 percent charge an additional fee for file extensions; 22 percent charge an additional fee for information received after a set deadline; and 24 percent charge an additional fee to expedite returns.[16]

3. It's Complicated

The federal tax code is just too darn complicated. Over the last century, the federal tax code has expanded dramatically in size and scope. In 1955, the Internal Revenue Code stood at 409,000 words.[17] Since then, it has grown to a total of 2.4 million words—almost six times as long as it was in 1955 and almost twice as long as in 1985, according to the Tax Foundation.[18]

However, the tax statutes passed by Congress are only the tip of the iceberg when it comes to tax complexity. There are roughly 7.7 million words of tax regulations, promulgated by the IRS over the last century, which clarify how US tax statutes work in practice. On top of that, there are almost sixty thousand pages of tax-related case law, which are indispensable for accountants and tax lawyers trying to figure out how much their clients actually owe.[19]

Taxes are complicated because there are competing goals for the tax system, and politics compounds complexity. Americans believe taxes should be fair, conducive to economic prosperity, enforceable, and simple. The problem is that the people who agree on those goals often disagree about the relative importance of each, according to an analysis from the Tax Policy Center, a program of the Urban Institute and Brookings Institution.[20] As a result, policies usually represent a balance among competing goals, and simplicity often loses out to other priorities.

Taxes have become so complicated that despite the increasing cost to file, most Americans still pay a tax professional to handle their taxes. Of the 69.5 million e-filing receipts for the 2016 tax year, more than half, or 37.1 million, came from tax professionals, according to the IRS's 2016 filing season statistics.[21]

If you do try to file taxes on your own, you may be disappointed if you call the IRS to ask a simple question. The phones will likely be jammed.

"Every filing season answering taxpayers' questions telephonically is on the agency's to-improve list," says Kay Bell, a blogger on taxes, in a February 15, 2018, blog post. "Last year, it even opened its phone lines on the Saturday (they usually take weekday-only calls) before the April filing deadline."[22]

Because of tax identity theft concerns, you'll first have to prove to the IRS that you are who you say you are. To ensure that IRS phone reps can be confident they are talking with legitimate taxpayers, the IRS is now asking both individual filers and the tax professionals who represent them to verify their identities when they call the IRS.

The time it takes to comply with the tax code imposes a real cost on the economy. Individuals and businesses need to devote resources to complying with the tax code instead of doing other productive activities. For example, a business owner who needs to file a complex tax return each year may hire an accountant or tax lawyer to do it. This tax professional may cost $70,000 a year or more. This is $70,000 that this business owner cannot devote to purchasing equipment or hiring workers. Economists refer to this as an opportunity cost, and it results in lost productivity. A simpler, more transparent tax code would benefit everyone.

4. It's Corrupted

Every tax filing season, examples of corruption become national headlines. In April 2017, a man was sentenced to twenty-four months in prison in Tampa, Florida, for falsely claiming to own the rights to landfill methane credits.[23] He was marketing the landfill methane credits to a network of tax return preparers for use on individual taxpayers' tax returns, despite knowing that the credits were nonexistent and not able to be claimed by the individual taxpayers. The total amount of false and fraudulent credits claimed in this case was estimated to be $4,211,757, a large portion of which was recovered from the individual taxpayers.

In March 2017, a Cleveland, Ohio, man was sentenced to twenty-six months in prison for falsely reporting that financial institutions had withheld large amounts of federal income tax on income that did not exist in reality. He falsely filed for tax refunds of $1,121,420 for tax years 2006 through 2011.[24]

In February 2017, an Alexandria, Virginia, man was sentenced to seven months in prison and one year of supervised release and ordered to pay $250,000 in restitution for conspiring to defraud the United States and to submit a false expatriation statement to the IRS. He also paid a civil penalty of $100 million to the US Treasury for failing to file and filing false Reports of Foreign Bank and Financial Accounts. His scheming started in 1995; by 2015, his offshore holdings hidden from the IRS exceeded $220 million.[25]

Those are just a few examples of individual taxpayers in one fiscal year who were actually caught. Undoubtedly, there are many, many more who've outwitted the system and haven't been caught.

We probably wouldn't have these tax evasion problems if we handled them the way the Apostle Peter dealt with Ananias and Sapphira in Acts 5:1–11. Go read the story. I'll bet nobody else in the first-century church lied about the money they collected from selling property. I'm just saying.

Even still, there are other examples of the federal government playing a role in subsidizing corruption. For example, look at how the federal government subsidizes housing through numerous tax and spending programs.

One of the more inefficient programs is the Low-Income Housing Tax Credit. The program provides $9 billion a year in tax credits to support housing construction, according to research from Chris Edwards and Vanessa Brown Calder for the Cato Institute.[26] The federal government distributes the credits to the states, which in turn award them to developers to cover part of the costs of constructing apartment buildings and other projects. In return, developers must cap rents for the units they set aside for low-income tenants.

The benefits of the Low-Income Housing Tax Credit are supposed to flow through to tenants in the form of lower rents, but studies suggest that investors, developers, and financial companies gain most of the benefits. The program has complex administration, is prone to abuse, and produces costly low-income housing. Any government program run by flawed human beings has this potential—another reason the best role of government is not to serve as a welfare state but to protect individual rights to enable people to defend and pursue their own welfare.

As lawmakers consider "major tax reforms aimed at reducing tax rates and ending unjustified tax breaks," writes Edwards and Calder in their report, they "should consider repealing the LIHTC [Low-Income Housing Tax Credit]. It complicates the tax code and is a poorly tar-geted solution to housing affordability problems."

Instead of federal subsidies, a better way to reduce housing costs would be through state and local policy reforms. The states should reduce the burden of building and zoning regulations to increase the supply of housing, including multifamily housing for low-income tenants. Easing up on regulation is almost always good for the people, as we'll see more a little later on.

5. It Hurts Our Global Standing

The United States finally reduced the federal corporate income tax rate from 35 percent to 21 percent with the recent Tax Cuts and Jobs Act.[27] Until then, we hadn't reduced our federal corporate income tax rate since the early 1990s. Our combined federal, state, and local corporate tax rate stood at around 39 percent, which is significantly higher than the average rate of 25 percent among nations belonging to the Organization for Economic Co-operation and Development, according to the Tax Foundation.[28]

Most nations that are part of the OECD have moved to a territorial tax system, while the United States has continued to tax the world-wide profits of its domestic corporations. If we're not careful, we'll be headed in the direction of France, which has introduced a number of reforms that have significantly increased marginal tax rates on work, saving, and investment. France also recently instituted a corporate income surtax, which joined other distortive taxes such as the financial transactions tax, a net wealth tax, and an inheritance tax, according to the Tax Foundation.[29]

It's imperative that we keep our tax policies attractive for business. In today's globalized world, capital is highly mobile. Business owners and investors have options. They can choose to invest in any number of countries throughout the world to find the highest rate of return. If a country's tax rate is too high, it will drive investment elsewhere, leading to slower economic growth. We see this on a smaller scale with Texas and California: a tax code that is competitive and neutral promotes sustainable economic growth and investment while raising sufficient revenue for government priorities. In the Tax Foundation's 2017 International Tax Competitiveness Index rankings, Estonia, New Zealand, and Switzerland top the list of thirty-five countries. Countries at the bottom include Portugal, Italy, and, lastly, France. Unfortunately, the United States is closer to this bunch, ranking at number thirty on the list.[30]

6. It Violates Privacy

The IRS issued a scam alert notice in February 2018 warning taxpayers of a quickly growing scam involving erroneous tax refunds being deposited into their bank accounts.[31] The IRS also offered a step-by-step explanation for how to return the funds and avoid being scammed.

Following up on a Security Summit alert issued on February 2, 2018, the IRS issued an additional warning about the new scheme after discovering more tax practitioners' computer files had been breached. In addition, the number of potential taxpayer victims jumped from a few hundred to several thousand in just days. The IRS Criminal Investigation Division is still investigating the scope and breadth of this scheme.

These criminals have a new twist on an old scam. After stealing client data from tax professionals and filing fraudulent tax returns, these criminals use the taxpayers' real bank accounts for the deposit. I know what you're thinking: "How can a stranger dropping money in my account be a bad thing?"

Well, the thieves are then using various tactics to reclaim the refund from the taxpayers, and their versions of the scam may continue to evolve.

In one version of the scam, criminals posing as debt collection agency officials acting on behalf of the IRS contact the taxpayers to say a refund was deposited in error, and they ask the taxpayers to forward the money to their collection agency.

In another version, the taxpayer who received the erroneous refund gets an automated call with a recorded voice that says it is from the IRS and threatens the taxpayer with criminal fraud charges, an arrest warrant, and a "blacklisting" of their Social Security number. The recorded voice gives the taxpayer a case number and a telephone number to call to return the refund.

The IRS urged taxpayers to follow established procedures for returning an erroneous refund to the agency. The IRS also encouraged taxpayers to discuss the issue with their financial institutions because there may be a need to close bank accounts.

The IRS also said that taxpayers who file electronically may find that their tax return will reject because a return bearing their Social Security number is already on file.

A complicated tax code makes law-abiding taxpayers easy game for these types of criminals. Simple taxes, easier to understand, also help protect citizens from scams.

On its own, Texas can't do much about the federal tax code. But conservative lawmakers who will fight for the tax principles that have made our economy so favorable to businesses and families can push back against unfair, complicated tax systems. And at home, we can guard against progressive socialists that would impose their own failed taxation systems on individuals that should be free to pursue the American Dream for themselves and their families.

I don't know about you, but I stand with Texas on taxes.

CHAPTER 6

LIVE AND LET LIVE

Minimal Regulation

In addition to one of the friendliest tax codes in the nation, Texas supports the businesses that support it by avoiding interfering, expensive overregulation. Texas follows the good ol' conservative principle of "live and let live." The people and the market can be darn good cops—and businesses that don't serve die. In my opinion, that's a sight better than killing them with choking regulations.

Many don't realize that regulatory compliance is expensive. On average, small-business owners nationally spend more than $83,000 in the first year of operation, then an additional $12,000 annually to stay compliant, according to recent survey data from the National Small Business Administration.[1]

Factored into those costs are attorney fees, workplace upgrades, and the time taken away from other tasks to understand regulations. One in three small-business owners spends more than eighty hours a year to meet compliance requirements.[2]

Over the course of five years, the average cost of a regulatory citation fine was $30,651, according to the SBA's survey conducted between November 28, 2016, and January 10, 2017.[3] More than half of the businesses surveyed had fewer than five employees and generated less than $5 million in annual sales.

"The impact of regulatory burden cannot be overstated. More than one-third have held off on business investment due to uncertainty on a pending regulation, and more than half have held off on hiring a new employee due to regulatory burdens," wrote Pedro Alfonso, NSBA chair, and Todd McCracken, NSBA president and CEO.[4]

To me, it's utterly incomprehensible why lawmakers would saddle the backbone of America with such an enormous weight. Why are they punishing small-business owners, who are the most consistent wealth generators of our country?

Our nation's small businesses generate three-fifths of net new jobs, accounting for a big chunk of US employment growth.[5] Small businesses employ 58 million people, or 48 percent of all private-sector employees, according to 2017 data from the US Small Business Administration's Office of Advocacy.[6]

These are businesses owned by Joe and Jane Six-Pack, those everyday Americans bootstrapping their operations from kitchen tables. Half of the nation's small businesses are home based, meaning they might have business activities outside the home, but the decision-making and core operations stem from the home, according to the SBA's data. About 22 percent of these business owners use personal and family savings to finance expansions.

But they're now showing signs of stress. Small businesses' share of the private nonfarm economy is slipping, and their employment and payroll growth is now lagging behind their larger counterparts. Economic studies support their concerns.[7] And if that's not clear enough, look no further than how and why they voted in the last presidential election.

So how do you revive small businesses and reverse their trajectory? You start by looking at the nation more granularly, at the state level, and observing what's working. When you do, you'll clearly see that Texas and other conservative states are more respectful of small business owners when it comes to regulations and thereby have stronger state economies.

Like many complex issues, there are several factors that influence small-business growth gaps across the nation. Yes, God-given traits such as geography and historical growth patterns matter, but leadership with character also matters. This includes minimalist tax policies and state regulatory policies.

"Those states that impose more costly regulations on small businesses should expect slower small business growth than states that impose less burdensome regulations," said Wayne Winegarden, PhD, in his white paper *The 50-State Small Business Regulation Index*.[8] "These adverse consequences are now heightened due to the current economic malaise that has taken a harsher toll on the nation's small businesses."

When regulations are tame and kept at bay, companies can flourish. Just look at D. R. Horton Inc., for example. Few companies have benefited more from Texas's conservative business principles than D. R. Horton Inc., the nation's largest homebuilder. The Arlington, Texas–based company reported revenue of $14.1 billion in fiscal year 2017, up a whopping 30 percent from 2015.[9]

Management consistently applies conservative business principles, making an effort to reduce both construction and selling and general and administrative expenses. In fiscal 2017, those expenses, as a percentage of homebuilding revenues, decreased 40 basis points to 8.9 percent.[10]

Donald R. Horton built his first neighborhood of affordable homes in the Dallas–Fort Worth region more than thirty years ago. The company grew from a local homebuilder to a regional homebuilder to ultimately the largest homebuilder in the United States.

Just before the recession, from 2000 to 2006, D. R. Horton's annual revenue quadrupled to around $15 billion.[11] It built around fifty-three thousand homes in 2006, up from just nineteen thousand at the beginning of the decade. The company's net income—its profits—jumped from $192 million in 2000 to more than $1.4 billion in 2006.

When the recession finally gripped the nation—from December 2007 through June 2009—D. R. Horton hit its meteoric rise. When other homebuilders folded, D. R. Horton seized the opportunity to gain market share.[12]

"It had to cut back like everybody else. But after the market hit bottom, the company knew where the cycle was," said Ted Wilson, principal of Residential Strategies, in a March 2011 article in *D CEO* magazine. "When the sun started rising again in the spring of 2009, it leaped in and made some deals."[13]

In addition, D. R. Horton's largest homebuilding markets are in conservative states like Texas, where the recession wasn't as pronounced. The Great Recession, as it's now called, was the worst since the 1929 Depression. The subprime mortgage crisis was the trigger, which created a global banking credit crisis. But Texas recovered from the recession faster because laws here make it harder for homebuyers to tap into their equity. Generally, we force homebuyers here to be more responsible. I saw firsthand how the subprime market impacted communities in Florida.

D. R. Horton is well positioned for the future. It now has the advantage of acquiring and developing land. In October 2017, D. R. Horton acquired 75 percent of outstanding shares for Austin, Texas–based Forestar Group Inc., a land developer. The acquisition, valued at $560 million, now gives D. R. Horton access to prime land and lot positions for its new home construction. With an impressive backlog worth $3.7 billion, along with a well-stocked supply of land, lots, and homes, D. R. Horton is well positioned for fiscal 2018.[14]

Texas supports businesses in a couple of key regulatory policies. These policies have helped Texan companies thrive.

Energy Regulations

One way in which states constrict the growth of small businesses is through the imposition of burdensome energy regulations. States handicap small businesses when they restrict the supply of energy, impose direct costs, and create production mandates. These regulations come in different forms. For instance, some states cap carbon dioxide emissions. Others impose consumption requirements such as a "revenue decoupling program."

I think liberal lawmakers sit in a room trying to come up with the cutest names possible for the most harmful regulations. Decoupling sounds sweet, but it's not. This socialistic move switches profit margins to the number of customers serviced rather than the total amount of power provided. It guarantees utilities earn a set amount of revenue by requiring small businesses to pay a higher rate on their electricity bills if demand falls. Revenue decoupling ensures that small business must pay a total electric bill that meets a state minimum level. This just adds to the collection of bills for Joe and Jane Six-Pack.

Excessive energy regulations can also stifle business growth. But in Winegarden's separate energy index, while New York ranks number fifty in terms of policies favorable for small-business growth, Texas ranks number one.[15] While the lower-ranked states saddle their small businesses with larger energy regulatory burdens, which have a direct link to energy costs, Texas's policies don't favor overregulation of energy, allowing its businesses some relief.

Tort Reform

Texas not only avoids passing legislation that burdens businesses but is active in promoting legislation to make things easier for professionals. Today, Texas is a top choice for business growth because of its fair legal system, but it wasn't always that way. Texas passed sweeping tort reform legislation in 2003 to curtail excessive malpractice lawsuits. Before that, lawsuits against doctors, malpractice insurance rates, and the number of medical professionals leaving the state skyrocketed. According to research from the Texas Public Policy Foundation:

- One out of every four doctors in Texas had a malpractice claim filed against him or her each year.
- 85 percent of all medical malpractice claims failed but still cost more than $50,000 to defend.
- The number of medical malpractice insurers in Texas dropped from seventeen in 2000 to only four in 2003. One of the four was the State of Texas as the insurer of last resort.
- Texas had one of the worst doctor-to-citizen ratios in the country, and it was getting worse.[16]

In June 2003, the state passed legislation to make the state's court system fair to ensure a fair market for business. Since then, malpractice insurance has become more affordable, doctors have returned to the state, and businesses now have one less hurdle to tackle when trying to grow their operations and provide care for their workers.

The Texas Public Policy Foundation compared Texas's approach to solving its medical malpractice rates with New York's approach. This case study is a succinct example of conservative and liberal approaches to a common issue. It has nothing to do with a state's traits—those natural blessings and challenges that you can't control—but everything to do with leadership characteristics.

In 2003, Texas physicians were paying about the same malpractice rates as New York physicians. Texas chose to adopt common-sense lawsuit reforms. As a result, the malpractice insurance premiums paid by Texas doctors fell by more than 60 percent on average. Most Texas doctors today are paying less than half of what they were paying before the reform.[17]

In contrast, malpractice premiums in New York have increased by 60 percent during the same period. As a result, almost two thousand physicians have moved their practices from New York to Texas, according to the foundation's research.[18]

New York needed a financial solution, so their liberal lawmakers resorted to their go-to fix—taxes. New York enacted legislation requiring the state to subsidize the malpractice insurance costs of doctors, ignoring the problems in the state's legal system that generated the high premium rates. This means that taxpayers in New York are paying New York trial lawyers through the conduit of frivolous medical malpractice lawsuits.

Encroaching Regulation in Texas

Despite Texas's history of avoiding and fighting burdensome regulation, however, thinking like New York's is spreading in the state. The city of Austin's burdensome regulations have already driven out companies like Uber and Lyft while putting pressure on companies like HomeAway and Airbnb. In San Antonio and West Lake Hills, you can't even cut trees on your own property.[19] In College Station, homeowners are practically banned from renting out their driveways on Aggie game day; that's no way to treat the 12th man.[20] In Denton, officials tried to ban fracking, but thankfully, it was overturned.[21]

Several states in this union already have become so inundated with a network of complicated tax rules and regulations that businesses have fled to Texas. But if Texas cities begin to pass more regulations like this, the state could transform into a place just like the onerous environments its businesses previously left. Texas can continue to support conservative principles by opposing progressive socialist regulation.

Avoiding Overregulation in Environmental Restrictions

Burdensome environmental restrictions limit development and eliminate jobs. Ever since the first major environmental regulations were established in the 1970s, there's been a looming worry among business leaders and conservative politicians that we could lose out to countries with environmental laws that aren't as strict or aren't followed as closely.

Whether the environmental regulation is at the state level, the federal level, or both, the additional costs force business leaders to make new decisions about pricing, production levels, and capital investments. Some companies pass costs on to customers, cut back production, or alter research and development plans. In either case, it creates a distortion in trade if companies in other countries don't have to carry the same burden.

Research shows that environmental policies, when carelessly applied, can unfairly impact corporate competitiveness. For example, an imbalance occurs when some firms are regulated while others are exempt. Some sectors will be required to face stricter pollution standards than others. Environmental stringency varies across jurisdictions.

That's one of the main problems I have with the United Nations Framework Convention on Climate Change's Paris Agreement that the previous president entered but from which our current administration wisely withdrew. Different countries are expected to take carbon mitigation action at different speeds. How is that fair to American manufacturers and their workers? If two competitors based in two different countries are given two different regulations to follow, someone's not getting a fair shake.

Whenever politicians pass environmental regulations, they typically mandate that the companies causing pollution must agree to stop certain manufacturing practices, which naturally creates a new cost for the companies. These environmental regulatory differences create changes in production costs, often directly.

Take the European Union Emissions Trading System, for example. It regulates carbon emissions for more than eleven thousand installations across Europe.[22] It's estimated that this Emissions Trading System has increased average material costs between 5 and 8 percent for companies in the iron, steel, power, and cement industries.[23]

How about an example closer to home? The US Clean Air Act Amendments of 1990 had no effect on the cement industry's marginal costs, but the average costs of entry increased.[24] The costs of building a new, greenfield facility increased by $5 million to $10 million due to the rigorous environmental certification and testing requirements of the Clean Air Act Amendments.

You also have to consider the differences in pollution abatement costs. Research from Carl Pasurka in the *Review of Environmental Economics and Policy* found that across nine countries in Europe, North America, and Asia, the amount of manufacturing capital spending devoted to pollution abatement in 2000 ranged from Taiwan's 1 percent to Canada's 5 percent.[25] I'm no math genius, but it appears that Taiwan had the advantage.

You also have to consider that abatement costs are naturally higher for industries prone to pollution—such as steel, pulp and paper, and oil refining. Each of these sectors in the United States spends around 1 percent of their revenue to comply with environmental regulations, while other manufacturing plants spent just 0.4 percent, according to research in the book *Does Regulation Kill Jobs?*, published in 2014.[26]

The previous White House administration took the stance that increased environmental regulations and more stringent policies would ignite investment in developing new pollution-reducing technologies. They believed that money saved as a result of these new technologies would more than offset any compliance costs. Many environmentalists credit this logic to research from Michael Porter and Claas van der Linde published in the *Journal of Economic Perspectives* in the fall of 1995.[27]

You'll often hear progressive socialists refer to environmental benefits as "public goods." That's a convenient verbal strategy for them. They'll claim that everyone benefits equally from these public goods that we all need. What a compelling argument. There's just one problem.

"Not everyone values public goods in the same way or by the same magnitude," writes Gary Libecap, senior fellow of the Hoover Institution and a professor of environmental policy. "Some citizens may strongly desire policies that for example, protect polar bears in the Artic. Others may not care at all."[28]

These different assessments of the value of public goods would not matter if providing them was inexpensive and advocates paid for them, but that's not the case, argues Libecap in his research entitled "The High Price of Environmental Regulations," published with the Hoover Institution.

Take it from a guy who has served time in Washington: politicians have little incentive to provide pure public goods. Why? You're not going to find lobbyists or key constituents getting out the vote and raising campaign donations if they aren't assured of receiving something special or if they aren't given some unique access or business leverage. True public goods go to everyone; in a sense, everyone gets a free ride with a true public good.

However, when a public good is especially valuable to a certain group of voters who are well financed and organized, then the politician has a different motive for being responsive. At this point, the public good is actually a masked private good. You'll see this playing out in environmental politics all the time.

Take the popularity over zero-emission vehicles, for example. Many states, following California's lead, aggressively push renewable fuels and zero-emission vehicles through subsidies. That's not so bad; I've never been opposed to clean energy. But here is where things get sour: California also raises the cost of power generation from fossil fuels to prop up the advantage of renewable fuels and zero-emission vehicles. That's like Five Guys—one of my favorite burger joints—trying to boost popularity of its new veggie sandwich by lowering the price of it by 50 percent but also raising the price of its classic cheeseburger by 50 percent. It wouldn't work.

The push for renewable fuels and zero-emission vehicles is part of an effort to reduce greenhouse gas emissions and mitigate possible climate change. However, one of the biggest problems with these clean energy policies is the lack of global cooperation to confront greenhouse gas internationally. How in the world is California going to single-handedly offset the noncompliance of China, India, Brazil, Indonesia, and every other country not participating in cross-national collaboration efforts on the environment?

By being so headstrong about pushing renewable fuels and zero-emission vehicles, states not only divert tax revenue from other uses, such as better schools, hospitals, and highways, but also raise consumer prices by increasing energy costs.

"Poorer tax payers often pay more of their incomes in taxes and consume more of their incomes, relative to wealthier citizens, who are the main members of environmental lobby groups and lobbyists for environmental regulation," Libecap says.

Consider Tesla, one of the more popular zero-emission automotive brands. The purchaser of each Tesla Model S that costs $70,000 or more receives a $7,500 federal tax credit, plus state credits.[29] Within California, for example, purchasers can get a tax rebate of up to $2,500 and the opportunity to access special freeway lanes, an important benefit in traffic-clogged California.[30] Moreover, the Tesla company receives four zero-emission vehicle credits, which it then sells to other car dealers in the state because the California Air Resources Board requires all dealers to sell a fixed number of zero-emission vehicles each year.[31] Because other car companies cannot meet that mandate given tepid demand, they must purchase credits from Tesla, effectively raising the costs of their cars and subsidizing Tesla.

Few inhabitants of South Central Los Angeles, one of the poorest parts of the city, can afford a Tesla. Those good, poor people probably don't know about Tesla's alleged environmental benefits or what each vehicle costs them. On the other hand, those in wealthier Brentwood and Beverly Hills have a far better sense of what they gain from a Tesla purchase.

"It is clear that low-income citizens are subsidizing the wealthy in this case, and as more and more state resources are devoted to such policies, the overall economy becomes less vibrant, generating fewer blue collar jobs and other opportunities for those who are struggling the most in the society," Libecap says. "For these people, an abstract notion of reducing GHG emissions and climate change in the face of worldwide free riding has little appeal."[32]

The wealthy and other related constituents who value efforts to confront climate change and bear few of the costs are strong supporters and lobbyists in the political arena.

Just check out the membership characteristics of the Natural Resources Defense Council, the Sierra Club, and Friends of the Earth. These individuals lobby politicians and regulatory agency officials (many of whom support an added mandate) to provide environmental public goods because they receive private benefits. They value the public goods more; they receive subsidies; and they pay relatively little of the costs.

The greater population is essentially being forced to go along with the passionate pet projects of the minority. Environmental regulation now consumes a growing share of the state and federal economy, and the problem is likely to get worse for two reasons.

First, most people don't have the time to object to the many environmental provisions being introduced. Think about it—the people who value environmental regulation the most are busy lobbying for it. However, those who value it the least are busy doing other things, like working, paying bills, taking care of their families, dealing with health care—you know, real-life stuff. There's no time in their schedule to be concerned about environmental policy. Wealthy advocates face fewer constraints.

To be sure, I do believe that even the poor care about basic environmental regulations, like safe parks for their children to play in, clean drinking water, and regular upkeep of local streams and lakes. Those are public goods everyone can get behind and support. But there are broader, more abstract causes, such as GHG controls or polar bear protections, which impact far less people. Don't believe me? Try going door to door in a working-class neighborhood asking for donations to save polar bears.

Public opinion polls rarely make clear what environmental policies will cost. This is the second reason why the problem of environmental regulation is likely to get worse: the costs are focused on the lowest-income citizens and are not transparent.

"It is hard for those parties to mobilize to demand careful scrutiny of environmental policies," Libecap says. "They care little about the environmental policies and know little about the costs they bear. For wealthy advocates, who benefit more and bear fewer costs, by contrast, there is every incentive to support regulation and to cloak the policies in broad public goods despite both harmful distributional and efficiency effects in the economy."

An illustrative example is the proposal to shield the Arctic National Wildlife Refuge in Alaska from oil exploration and production by declaring the region wilderness. The presidential executive order made in January 2015 covers nearly 13 million acres, slightly smaller than the state of West Virginia.[33] The objective is to protect pristine habitat, home to caribou, polar bears, birds, and marine life, from any disruptions caused by oil and gas development. The January 27, 2015, *New York Times* editorial applauded this effort by the Obama administration as protecting a "valued wilderness."[34]

Fair enough. But how valuable? At what cost? And who benefits and bears those costs? These are critical questions in assessing whether or not this action to provide an environmental public good is broadly beneficial for the American public. Would the policy stand public scrutiny if the costs and benefits and their distribution were put up to public debate? Because less-educated, lower-income citizens are less likely to vote or to join lobby groups, they are underrepresented in political lobbying relative to citizens who are more educated and wealthier.

All in all, environmental regulation, which is replacing price and entry controls as the most prevalent form of government regulation, is growing. It is generally applauded because it provides public goods.

In many cases, it might. In other cases, the benefits are largely private goods, despite the way in which the policies are described. The problem arises because of the lack of balance in who pays for these policies and who values the benefits from them. Advocates, who are proficient in the political arena, get more and pay less. General citizens, who are much less proficient, get fewer policies that they value and pay more.

Measuring the true impact of environmental regulations is challenging because trying to account for other variables, such as the basic business acumen of a company's leaders or the stringency of other regulations a company has to follow, is difficult. To truly measure the impact of any environmental regulation, you really need to find a specific area where there's clear-cut data directly connected to the environmental regulation.

Let's take a look at one particular burdensome regulation from the US Environmental Protection Agency. The EPA recently set National Ambient Air Quality Standards for common air pollutants. The EPA says these air pollutants—ground-level ozone, carbon monoxide, sulfur oxides, nitrogen oxides, and lead—are found all over the United States. The EPA has set limits for how many of these pollutants are allowed to be in the air. A geographic area that meets or does better than the EPA's standard is called an "attainment" area. However, geographic areas with too many of these common pollutants are classified as "nonattainment" areas.[35] Got it? Good.

Now let's see how this one EPA air quality regulation plays out in a specific community. The Texas Commission on Environmental Quality commissioned a study to determine the financial impact of Central Texas's recent nonattainment designation. The study found that the EPA's nonattainment designation will cost the Austin–Round

Rock region between $24 and $41 billion between 2018 and 2046. On an annual basis, that would be an average of a little more than $1 billion per year.[36]

Those are big numbers, so let me break down how they arrived at those costs with a few examples that we can all grasp. Samsung Austin Semiconductor is a semiconductor manufacturing facility in Travis County, which is part of the Central Texas nonattainment region. Samsung's facility represents approximately $13.6 billion in capital investments.[37] An official from Samsung has indicated that it expects to expand up to an additional $13.6 billion through 2025, but this investment would very likely not occur if the region is designated nonattainment by the EPA.[38] Why is that, Lt. Col. West? Well, I'm glad you asked. Simply put, Samsung has other options. The company has about twenty other manufacturing plants worldwide where it could divert the expansion. If the EPA's burdensome air quality regulation restricts construction in the Central Texas region, Samsung will build its plant elsewhere. And frankly, I don't blame Samsung for finding more economical places to build their products. They'd be crazy not to do so. If they expanded as planned in Austin, it would add the equivalent of fifteen hundred to twenty-five hundred jobs to the facility, according to the report from the Texas Commission on Environmental Quality.[39]

How about another example? A new cement plant proposed for either Hays, Travis, or Williamson County in Central Texas also could be scratched because of the EPA's nonattainment designation.[40] Right now, all the cement plants in Texas are located along the I-35 corridor from Bexar County up to Ellis County because that's where the raw material needed for cement production is located. Of the five metro areas located along this corridor—Dallas–Fort Worth, San Antonio, Austin–Round Rock, Killeen-Temple, and Waco—the Austin–Round Rock area has the lowest ozone design value and would be in the best position to avoid being designated nonattainment. It also happens to be the fastest-growing region in the state, leading to a higher demand for cement products than slower-growing parts of the state. However, based on conversations between the Texas Cement Council and Texas Lehigh Cement Company, regional officials believe that the nonattainment designation would preclude the construction of a new cement plant in the region.[41]

The Capital Area Council of Governments—which represents Central Texas counties—estimated the investment for a new cement plant to be between $306 million and $713 million.[42] The impact on the local economy of the construction phase would be between $232 million and $542 million. The Capital Area Council of Governments then estimated the impact of the lost revenue over twenty years from the expansion failing to be built. Using operational data from Texas Lehigh Cement Company, their proposed one-million-ton cement plant expansion would contribute $1.6 billion to the local economy over a twenty-year period of new sales in the cement manufacturing sector.[43] If Lehigh Cement company opted for a two-million-ton cement plant, it could translate into more than $3.2 billion over a twenty-year period. We're talking real money and jobs lost because of a simple EPA air quality designation.

Those are just two examples of lost investment from 2018 through 2046 from scratched projects, but there are other costly penalties of the poor air quality designation to consider, too. The region still has to spend millions upon millions of dollars conforming to the EPA's standards.[44] And after conforming, the Texas Transportation Institute says it would lose money from things like road construction project delays during compliance tests.[45]

In order to continue to support prolabor policies, Texas should be ready to fight for only those environmental regulations that protect true public goods, not the pet projects of well-funded private interest groups. By all means, keep our parks clean and our water pure and support clean energy. But leave the expensive regulations that shut down business at the store.

Avoiding Overregulation in the Workplace

Excessive government regulation can also be a major stumbling block in the workplace itself. I'll highlight a handful of regulations that have undermined business growth—patterns of thinking we Texans need to fight against if we're going to stay the Friendly State for our businesses.

State Licensing Requirements

I can totally understand why doctors, police officers, and pilots need to be licensed. I wouldn't dare step on a plane with an unlicensed pilot. But tell me, why do low-risk occupations like African hair braiders need to have a license? Right now, thirteen states require braiders to obtain a full cosmetology license.[46] Braiders are regulated as hairstylists, hairdressers, or cosmetologists. The onerous course requirements range from a thousand-hour hairstylist course in Wyoming to twenty-one hundred hours needed to become a licensed cosmetologist in South Dakota.[47]

It makes no sense that a safe practice of simply braiding hair—with no dyes or chemicals—has been going on for more than a thousand years, but certain state governments feel it's now necessary to regulate it.

A few states are changing their rules. In June 2018, a new stand-alone braiding license was signed into law, finally allowing natural, African-style hair braiders in Missouri to practice their art without a cosmetology license.[48] Average tuition for those licenses in Missouri was upward of $12,000. With the new license, however, braiders can simply pay a $20 fee and watch a four- to six-hour video.[49] If ever I decided to alter my salt-and-pepper flattop, I'd feel totally comfortable going to any one of these non-cosmetology-licensed hair braiders.

Others with similarly low-risk occupations, like interior designers, tree trimmers, and tour guides, must also overcome the financial burdens of a license.

On February 27, 2018, subcommittee chairman Dave Brat (R-VA) and the Subcommittee on Economic Growth, Tax and Capital Access held a hearing on occupational licensing and its excessive impact on American small businesses.

"The percentage of the workforce that requires an occupational license has increased from less than 5 percent in the 1950s to almost 33 percent today," Brat said. "But one of the most telling statistics about licensing is that while there are 1,100 occupations in the United States that are licensed in at least one state, only 60 require a license in all 50 states. This inconsistency hurts worker mobility and most importantly, small businesses."[50]

Despite small-business confidence reaching an all-time high, many see burdensome licensing regulations as another barrier small-business owners must overcome.

"I'm not prepared to say that licensing should go away. I need the foundation and the commitment. Let's create reform where appropriate to better fit the current realities of trades and professions," said Frank Zona, owner of Zona Salons in Norwell, Massachusetts, testifying on behalf of the Professional Beauty Association.[51]

"Some licensing requirements are necessary, but what has become evident in our own research is that for many of our members, nearly 68 percent in our snapshot poll, said that they find that the licensing requirements hinder their ability to operate their small business," said Keith Hall, president and CEO of the National Association for the Self-Employed in Annapolis Junction, Maryland.[52]

"Occupational licensure acts as a formidable barrier to entry for low- and middle-income Americans seeking to enter new professions," said C. Jarrett Dieterle, senior fellow at the R Street Institute in Washington, DC. "The result is a government-imposed barrier that arbitrarily limits Americans' ability to work and climb the income ladder to more prosperity."[53]

"Evidence indicates that occupational licensing can hamper mobility, making it harder for workers to take advantage of job opportunities in other regions," said Dr. Morris Kleiner, professor at the University of Minnesota in Minneapolis, Minnesota. "Overall, occupational licensing and the lack of consistency across state borders with respect to the education and training of licensed practitioners can carry broad implications for the economic well-being of individuals."[54]

Fiduciary Rule for Investment Advisors

The Department of Labor's fiduciary rule for investment advisors has been put on hold for further review, and rightfully so.[55] The impact would be painful for the financial advisory industry, low- to middle-income citizens, and small-business owners.

The fiduciary rule was initially created under the Obama administration as part of a major push for transparency in the financial industry. It was part of a sweeping set of reforms proposed in the wake of the Great Recession of 2008.

In short, the Department of Labor's definition of a fiduciary demands that retirement advisors act in the best interests of their clients and put their clients' interests above their own. The fiduciary rule is essentially a promise that financial advisors must be honest about their own commissions with clients.

In announcing the rule on February 23, 2015, President Obama said: "Today, I'm calling on the Department of Labor to update the rules and requirements that retirement advisors put the best interests of their clients above their own financial interests. It's a very simple principle: You want to give financial advice, you've got to put your client's interests first."[56]

The problem with the rule is that it comes with unintended consequences. The rule adds to the growing cost of compliance. It would drive many financial advisors out of the low-to-middle-income investing market. Investors would have less advice and fewer resources to make informed choices about their retirement funds.

Look, I'm not naïve. I know there are opportunists—even straight-up crooks—in the financial industry. In IRAs alone, biased advice is costing American working families about $17 billion per year, according to a 2015 report from the White House Council of Economic Advisers.[57] The typical worker can lose a lot to conflicted advice.

Let's say a financial company rewards your advisor for recommending investments with high fees. You follow the recommendation, and as a result, you pay 1 percent more in fees every year than would have been ideal. So instead of earning, say, 6 percent each year, your nest egg earns 5 percent. It may seem like a small difference, and you might not suspect that you're paying too much. Over time, that difference adds up. If you roll over $100,000 from your 401(k) into an IRA earning 6 percent, in ten years it will have grown to $179,000. But if you follow conflicted advice, pay an extra 1 percent, and earn only 5 percent, your $100,000 will grow to just $163,000. Your advisor's conflict of interest just cost you $16,000. And as more time passes, your losses grow faster.

But whatever happened to researching and simply asking questions before signing your name? I'm going to go out on a limb and say that Americans are capable of asking questions to get clarity before handing over their money.

This is another classic case of progressive socialists turning us into a nanny state, in which the government becomes overprotective by interfering with personal choice. Quite honestly, all the fiduciary rule would do is force the financial industry to find creative ways around the rule, while still passing the new compliance cost on to customers. States like Texas should stand up and say no to the fiduciary rule.

Reporting Pay Data by Gender and Race

On July 14, 2016, the US Equal Employment Opportunity Commission published a proposal to collect summary pay data by race, ethnicity, and gender from employers with one hundred or more workers.[58]

Data collection and reporting was to start in March 2018, but the Trump administration announced in August 2017 that it would stop the regulation from being carried out.[59]

I'm fully aware of bias and discrimination, but reporting pay data by gender and race isn't going to fix the problem. It would have the unintended consequence of compromising employee privacy, not to mention increasing the paperwork burden on businesses. And even when the data is submitted, it could be misleading. Some pay disparities are in place for good reason, such as training, seniority, or the amount of overtime worked.

To EEOC's credit, they at least acknowledged in their July 2016 written proposal that the data collection likely would cost employers some money. In an explanatory document on its website, the agency says: "The EEOC estimates that the addition of pay data will increase the annual cost for time spent completing the report by about $416 per employer, totaling about $25 million for all employers who must file it. This is an estimate; some employers will have higher annual costs and others will have lower annual costs."[60]

Well, what did employers have to say about it? In a March 20, 2017, letter to John "Mick" Mulvaney, director of the Office of Management and Budget, twenty-seven industry associations—from the National Association of Manufacturers to the National Council of Chain Restaurants—complained about the proposed onerous requirement in detail:

"This expansion means huge additional costs for companies of all sizes, yet has no accompanying benefit, or protections for the confidentiality of the information to be gathered under the revised government form.

"Although reporting of the new information does not begin for approximately one year, employers are already making the necessary investments in software upgrades, internal reporting processes, and staffing needs in order to comply."[61]

I'm not a mathematician, but that sounds an awful lot more than $416 per employer.

In their letter, the industry associations cited the EEOC's violation of the Paperwork Reduction Act as a reason that the data collection and reporting regulation should be rejected. If carried out, the form employers would have been required to complete would have been expanded from 180 to 3,660 data cells. "By itself, this exponential increase in the amount of solicited data speaks volumes with regard to the burdensome nature of the new EEO-1 form," employers said.[62]

Nancy Hammer, senior government affairs policy counsel at the Society for Human Resource Management, a global business group with 270,000 members, said the expanded data-collection process lacked specificity to find evidence of discrimination.

"We didn't think it would help them solve the issue they were trying to solve, which is rooting out pay discrimination," Hammer said in an August 30, 2017, article for the *Washington Post*. "Pay has a lot of variables, and the way they collected the data was in pretty big categories."[63]

Hammer said wage disparities remain a problem in the United States. She recommends that employees go to their human resources department if they're concerned about their paycheck, giving their employer a chance to explain or fix the issue.

Otherwise, Hammer said, "To really do it, you'd need to practically report on every single employee. That's not a practical way of looking at this issue nationwide."

The Joint Employer Standard

In addition to bad laws that would impact employee privacy without truly solving pay discrimination, progressive socialists are considering imposing further interfering regulations on American businesses. The National Labor Relations Board recently made changes to a regulation that now opens the door for an employer to suddenly be responsible for all labor-law violations and collective-bargaining obligations of a contractor or franchisee.[64]

The regulation is known as the joint employer standard. Basically, it says that when businesses are in a contractual relationship wherein they both have control and responsibility over a certain group of employees, both must share the responsibilities of each other's workplace.

At first glance, it may not sound all that bad, but you have to think in terms of a larger business now being on the hook for problems occurring with a contractor. Employers will be forced to think twice about providing any assistance to small companies they contract with in order to avoid greater liability.

"This includes taking down online job posting portals and no longer supplying scheduling software and guidance on employment issues," research from the Competitive Enterprise Institute points out. "Among the hardest hit will be franchise businesses, which will have to spend more time and resources on activities for which their franchisor previously offered assistance."[65]

The Competitive Enterprise Institute estimates that the NLRB's new joint employer standard would put at risk at least forty thousand small businesses operating in more than seventy-five thousand locations.

The rule essentially means that a franchisor can now be dragged into a franchisee's employment-based legal disputes, causing increased costs for everyone—higher operational costs, greater exposure to litigation, and increased liability insurance premiums. To avoid becoming entangled in legal disputes, the Competitive Enterprise Institute says large companies may also steer clear of contracting with small businesses entirely. If done on a large scale, many small businesses would lose valuable clients critical to their survival.

Also, consider this: What's the appeal of being an entrepreneur if there's a rule that says you no longer have autonomy and flexibility to be your own boss? Many entrepreneurs do not have the necessary knowledge or resources to start their own operations, but with assistance from a franchisor parent company—including management best practices, branding, and marketing—they have the opportunity to succeed as franchise business owners.

You simply can't keep creating barriers for small businesses. Our country's financial health depends on their ability to create jobs for others. Small-business startups have created 66 percent of net new jobs since the 1970s, according to data from the US Small Business Administration.[66]

The NLRB made its definition changes to "joint employer" status on August 27, 2015, as part of a ruling on a case involving Browning-Ferris Industries of California, a recycling management company.[67] Browning had a contract with Leadpoint Business Services, which provided workers for sorting, housekeeping, and screen-cleaning tasks. In June 2013, a workers' union filed a petition with the NLRB in Oakland, California, seeking to represent a unit of all sorters, housekeepers, and screen cleaners at the Browning facility, excluding

Browning's own directly employed workers, who were unionized under a different union contract. In their petition to the NLRB, the union claimed that Leadpoint and Browning jointly employed the sorters, housekeepers, and screen cleaners. The NLRB's decision came down to whether Browning and Leadpoint were joint employers or whether Leadpoint was the sole employer of the contracted employees.

From the union's standpoint, they would prefer that the employees belong to the much larger Browning, because it would give them more leverage and opportunity to grow their membership.

In its decision, the NLRB found that Browning was a joint employer with Leadpoint.[68]

The ruling was briefly overturned in March 2018 after the current White House administration appointed new members to the NLRB, but the victory was short lived. A motion was filed and granted to reinstate the initial ruling.[69]

This issue is not likely to go away soon. It's just another example of how progressive socialists have pushed for regulations and changes that make it harder on small businesses to thrive, which directly impacts the health of the nation.

Independent Contractor Test

Another government regulation hurting entrepreneurs is the task of proving a worker is an independent contractor. On the surface, it seems that as long as the employer and worker agree to the terms of their relationship, that's all that should matter. Unfortunately, that makes too much sense. So how about we throw some regulation in the mix, just to make it complicated for entrepreneurs trying to grow their businesses? Sounds fair, right?

State and federal governments care a lot about how workers are classified because it impacts how much money they can collect in taxes. If a worker has contract status, the company doesn't pay taxes and has fewer legal obligations. It's a beneficial arrangement for small companies trying to get off the ground and for larger companies trying to simply contain operational costs.

"An employer can save approximately $3,710 per worker per year in employment taxes on an annual average of $43,007 in income paid per employee when the employer misclassifies a worker as an independent contractor," a June 14, 2013, report from the US Treasury Inspector General's Office reported during the Obama administration.[70] The Internal Revenue Service estimates that employers have misclassified millions of workers nationally as independent contractors.[71]

There are several different independent contractor tests to determine a worker's status. If an employer hires someone without taking into consideration the requirements of various state and federal agencies, they could be on the hook for audits, fines, and additional taxes.

Our friends at the IRS are the most difficult people to satisfy. According to the IRS, the facts that provide evidence of independent contractor status fall into three categories:

- Behavioral: Does the company control or have the right to control the worker as well as how the worker does his or her job? For example, if a company provides training for the worker, this signals an expectation to follow company guidelines and therefore indicates that the worker is likely an employee.

- Financial: Are the business aspects of the worker's job controlled by the payer? (These include things like how a worker is paid, whether expenses are reimbursed, who provides tools, supplies, etc.). Only an independent contractor can realize a profit or incur a financial loss from his or her work.

- Type of relationship: Are there written contracts or employee-type benefits (i.e., a pension plan, insurance, vacation pay, etc.)? Will the relationship continue, and is the work a key aspect of the business?[72]

  •

The issue of who has the right to control is often not clear cut, and the tax code does not define "employee." Businesses must weigh all these factors when determining whether a worker is an employee or independent contractor.

The legal ramifications are huge:

- In April 2016, Uber decided to settle a class-action lawsuit brought against it by drivers in California and Massachusetts for $100 million. Because the case did not go to trial, the independent contractor dispute question has not yet been resolved.[73]
- In April 2015, the Department of Labor announced that it recovered $700,000 in back wages, damages, and penalties for over one thousand misclassified construction industry workers in Utah and Arizona.[74]
- In September 2014, the Sacramento Superior Court in California ruled that the *Sacramento Bee* misclassified over fifty-one hundred newspaper carriers as independent contractors.[75]
- In May 2013, the Department of Labor helped 196 employees at a Kentucky-based cable installer recover over $1 million in retroactive overtime pay and other benefits.[76]
- In 2012 and 2013, after having hired three hundred additional investigators, the Department of Labor collected more than

$18.2 million in back wages on behalf of nineteen thousand employees who had been misclassified.[77]

- Two separate class-action lawsuits launched by exotic dancers resulted in multi-million-dollar settlements for the employees long misclassified as independent contractors. The litigation in both cases was lengthy; however, this could prove useful in establishing precedent for other misclassified employees in an industry where it appears misclassification is common practice. Going forward, the employers involved in the suits will no longer classify dancers as independent contractors but as either employees or shareholders.[78]

Proving the distinction between an independent contractor and an employee can be expensive and onerous for both parties involved. Conservatives should do their part to protect businesses and their workers by opposing overregulation.

Overtime Rules

Under the Obama administration, on May 18, 2016, the Labor Department released a new rule on overtime that would have forced employers to pay workers overtime if they earn less than $47,476 a year.[79] That would have been a whopping 101 percent increase from the previous overtime threshold of $23,660.[80] In addition to raising costs for employers, which discourages hiring, the new overtime rule would have prevented employees from having flexible work schedules.

As you might imagine, the rule would have been the death knell for employers of all sizes. A month after the proposed rule was announced, entrepreneurs lined up for a chance to express their frustration with the Small Business Committee in the US House of Representatives.

Adam Robinson, CEO and cofounder of Hireology, a Chicago-based human resources software company, told the committee that if the rule had been in place when he started his company, he wouldn't even have been able to hire his first employee.

"My company now has 100 employees with a median annual compensation that exceeds $70,000 a year—well above the US average. How many 'Hireology's' won't get started as a result of this rule making that 1st employee unaffordable for an entrepreneur? Are fewer good-paying jobs created and fewer businesses launched the outcomes that are desired here?" Robinson asked the committee.[81]

Sales professionals—the lifeblood of almost every company—also would have suffered from this rule because their commission-based compensation structure doesn't align with the Department of Labor's vision of the workplace.

"Consider what my company is facing: Forty of our 100 full-time salaried professionals are salespeople, whose success—like with most sales positions—depends on persistence. That means working until the sale is made, whatever the hours," Robinson said during his June 23, 2016, testimony. "We pay new salespeople a base salary of $40,000, and those who hit their quota can earn $70,000 to $120,000 a year. This compensation structure is typical in the technology and sales sectors because it allows employees to directly share in the profits they produce for the company."

Testimonies similar to Robinson's from other business owners were followed up with lawsuits from several state and business-centric organizations. Eventually, all the lawsuits were consolidated into a single case in the US District Court for the Eastern District of Texas. Good ol' Texas conservatives drew a line in the sand and an injunction was granted to halt implementation of the new rules. An appeal of the injunction was filed, but the case continued, and the plaintiffs moved for a summary judgment. On August 31, 2017, a judge ruled that the Department of Labor exceeded its authority with the new overtime rules.[82] The Department of Labor finally dismissed its appeal, effectively ending the litigation.

The updated overtime rule never passed, but don't think for a New York minute that it won't pass in the near future. Proponents of the rule change are certainly licking their chops for another opportunity.

Fighting Regulation

Texas has a history of conservative policies that protect business from burdensome regulation that cuts into profit margins, chokes creativity and freedom, and impedes startups. Progressive socialists don't believe people will protect what matters to them. They don't believe people can even protect themselves from unscrupulous business practices. I say, if there's one thing you can always count on, it's that people will look out for number one.

Progressive socialists think Texas should get in line with the nanny-state mentality—the same mentality that has doctors packing up the practice to head to Texas and airlines breathing a sigh in relief to be someplace that lets them do their job and make a living without all that regulatory stress. I say, the same kind of people that fought at the Alamo will fight for their rights to run their businesses and live their lives free of progressive socialist interference and regulation.

CHAPTER 7

SOUTHERN HOSPITALITY

Probusiness Policies

With its low taxes and favorable regulations, Texas takes the Hippocratic Oath to "first, do no harm" to businesses. But its architects also understand that when luring jobs to the state, it's easier fishing with good bait. For so many companies, Texas is on the short list of potential relocation destinations because of its tax incentives, financial assistance, and a suite of services at the ready. Texas doesn't settle for getting rid of harmful policies; we make our state actively inviting to businesses and families.

The Texas Enterprise Fund is designed specifically to close corporate deals. The idea is to send a strong message that if you're good for Texas, we will compete to earn your business. The Texas Enterprise Fund is a financial incentive for companies planning a new facility opening or expansion, with significant projected job creation. It's used especially in cases where Texas is in competition with another out-of-state option. That's taking a William B. Travis attitude to job creation.

Deal-closing cash grants are calculated for each applicant. Award amounts are based on the average wage of new employees, taking into account the expected hiring timeline and number of jobs created.

Among the requirements is that a company must demonstrate significant levels of planned capital investment.

From fiscal year 2004, when the incentive was first offered, through April 2018, Texas invested $618 million, according to the state's records.[1] I call it an investment because for a little more than half a billion dollars, we gained 93,800 jobs and cumulative capital investments of $27 billion.[2]

That's not all. We offer a Texas Enterprise Zone Program, Product Development and Small Business Incubator Fund, Texas Leverage Fund, industrial revenue bonds, and a capital access program. There's even a Spaceport Trust Fund to support the development of a spaceport where a reusable launch vehicle or spacecraft can be located.

A Right-to-Work Leader

Texas not only actively invites businesses here but leads the nation in enacting business-friendly policies. Right-to-work laws—which prohibit union activity from being a required condition of employment—originated here in Texas.

Winegarden's index compares all fifty states based on the impact from each state's regulatory environment on small businesses. Among the key findings is that none of the lowest-ranked ten states in the index—California, Connecticut, Hawaii, Maine, New Jersey, New York, Oregon, Rhode Island, Vermont, and Washington—are right-to-work states. Right-to-work laws have a statistically significant and positive impact on economic growth. And states that have right-to-work laws experience faster growth, according to research from the Buckeye Institute in the white paper *Ohio Right-to-Work: How the Economic Freedom of Workers Enhances Prosperity.*[3]

Unions gained political protection when president Franklin Roosevelt signed into law the National Labor Relations Act in July 1935. According to Roosevelt, the act protected "the right of self-organization of employees in industry for the purposes of collective bargaining."[4] The law imposed a duty on employers to engage in collective bargaining with unions and imposed a duty on workers to pay those negotiating unions under union security agreements.

That didn't sit well with the new "oillionaires" in Texas. They fought vigorously to defeat Roosevelt in upcoming elections. As mentioned earlier, John Henry Kirby, an early Texas lumber and oil tycoon who lost his fortune in the Great Depression, created several political organizations to fight Roosevelt, namely the Southern Committee to Uphold the Constitution. One of Henry's key partners was Vance Muse, the Texas conservative lobbyist who started the right-to-work movement against the unionization of American workers and helped pass the first antiunion laws in Texas. The term "right to work" was actually coined by *Dallas Morning News* editorial writer William Ruggles on Labor Day in 1941.[5]

By 1947, members of Congress proposed changes to the prounion structure of the NLRA and, over the veto of president Harry Truman, passed the Taft–Hartley Act, which restricted the power of unions to override minorities in the workplace and run over entrepreneurs.

Progressive Socialist Efforts to Strengthen Unions

Right-to-work laws strengthen the economy, while unchecked labor unions can weaken it. History has supported this, and Americans are recognizing it. In 2016, there were 14.6 million union members in the United States, down from 17.7 million in 1983.[6] The percentage of workers belonging to a union in the United States, or total labor union density, was 10.7 percent, compared to 20.1 percent in 1983, according to the Bureau of Labor Statistics.[7] Union membership in the private sector has fallen under 7 percent—levels not seen since 1932.

Today, workers in the public sector account for most of the union's membership rolls. Even though membership across the nation has dropped considerably, the services that involve the most vulnerable in our society—our children, hospital patients, passengers on a plane—still are in the grips of unions.

Progressive socialists fail to understand how our management of unions impacts our global standing. Being unable to maintain an environment where businesses and social services can succeed is a sign of weak leadership. President Ronald Reagan understood that thirty-six years ago when he threatened to fire nearly thirteen thousand air traffic controllers unless they called off an illegal strike.

President Reagan's decision in 1981 against the Professional Air Traffic Controllers Organization, or Patco, single-handedly undercut the bargaining power of that union, sent a message to other federal workers, and let the Soviet Union know how tough he could be.

"His forceful handling of the walkout, meanwhile, impressed the Soviets, strengthening his hand in the talks he later pursued with Mikhail S. Gorbachev," read a *New York Times* editorial on the anniversary of the decision.[8]

It's interesting how Reagan himself evolved; in 1947, Reagan was elected president of the Screen Actors Guild. In 1960, he led that union in a strike against production companies that forever changed the fortunes of tens of thousands of film actors. But despite these achievements, as president, he recognized the impact unions can have on a nation's economy.

Today, organized labor's primary concern is to pass the Employee Free Choice Act. It's an interesting name because the legislation would allow union organizers to harass and pressure workers to join the union. Traditional union elections happen through a secret ballot; the Employee Free Choice would involve publicly signed cards.

Supporters of the legislation—which, by the way, has failed numerous times to gain support, even from Democrats—argue that bill would make it easier for unions to organize workers. They say unions are necessary to protect the middle class with higher wages.

Unions argue that they can raise their members' wages, but few Americans understand the economic theory explaining how they do this, writes James Sherk in a report for the Heritage Foundation. "Unions are labor cartels," Sherk says. "Cartels work by restricting the supply of what they produce so that consumers will have to pay higher prices for it."[9]

OPEC is probably the best-known such cartel. It attempts to raise the price of oil by cutting oil production. As labor cartels, unions attempt to monopolize the labor supplied to a company or an industry in order to force employers to pay higher wages. Cartels benefit their members in the short run but eventually harm the economy.

Politicians at the highest level couldn't understand it. President Barack Obama supported the Employee Free Choice Act. In fact, he was an original cosponsor of the Employee Free Choice Act. He urged his Senate colleagues to pass the bill during a 2007 motion to proceed:

> I support this bill because in order to restore a sense of shared prosperity and security, we need to help working Americans exercise their right to organize under a fair and free process and bargain for their fair share of the wealth our country creates.
>
> The current process for organizing a workplace denies too many workers the ability to do so. The Employee Free Choice Act offers to make binding an alternative process under which a majority of employees can sign up to join a union. Currently, employers can choose to accept—but are not bound by law to accept—the signed decision of a majority of workers. That choice should be left up to workers and workers alone.

"I will make it the law of the land when I'm president of the United States," Obama told a labor federation meeting in April 2008. In another speech to the AFL-CIO in 2010, Obama vowed to keep fighting for the bill.

Automotive Unions

An illustrative example of how unions work: What if Chrysler, Ford, and General Motors all agreed to raise the price of the cars they sold by $4,000? Their profits would also jump from every American who bought a car at the new higher price. Some Americans wouldn't be able to afford the vehicles at the higher price, and the automakers would make and sell fewer vehicles. If that were the case, they would then need fewer workers. Chrysler, Ford, and GM would make more money and benefit from a higher stock price in the short run, but the economy would eventually suffer.

"That is why federal antitrust laws prohibit cartels and the automakers cannot collude to raise prices," Sherk says.

Of course, the idea is flawed. These days, Americans will simply buy a more reasonably priced Toyota, Honda, Hyundai, Kia, etc.

But believe it or not, autoworker unions have routinely applied such pressure to improve the salaries of laborers—pressure that eventually backfired. The United Auto Workers, which represents the autoworkers in Detroit, routinely went on strike unless the manufacturers paid what they demanded. Countless stories have been written about how the gold-plated UAW health benefits for retirees and active workers added $1,200 to the cost of each vehicle that GM produced in 2007. Can you imagine how that puts the automaker at a competitive disadvantage? Back in 1987, the UAW even secured a Jobs Bank program, which essentially prevented the companies from laying off workers without pay; thousands of union members would receive full pay for literally showing up to the job site, sitting in a room, and doing nothing for eight hours.

According to the rules of the Jobs Bank program, which ended in 2009, no eligible employee could be laid off over the term of the agreement, except under the following specific circumstances:

- Reduced customer demand, a maximum of forty-two weeks over the life of the agreement (commonly known as loss of market share);

- Acts of God or other conditions beyond the control of management;
- Conclusion of an assignment known in advance to be temporary; and
- Plant rearrangement or model changeover.

Eligible employees could not be laid off because of new technology (robots), sourcing decisions, or company-implemented efficiency actions, according to details of the original agreement shared with the Truth About Cars website.

The UAW negotiated different types of layoffs. There were temporary layoffs, where workers would know their return date, and indefinite layoffs, where workers would get forty-two weeks of unemployment benefits and a supplemental from their employer equal to 100 percent of their salary. After forty-two weeks, workers would be reemployed by the Jobs Bank, at which time they would receive 95 percent of their salary. They didn't get seniority, but they did continue to receive health benefits. While in protected status, employees could be assigned to training programs, certain nontraditional jobs, openings at other UAW locations (they only had to accept them if the job was within one hundred miles of their home; otherwise, they could stay in jobs banks), and other assignments "consistent with the intent of the program."

Unions' role as monopoly cartels explains their opposition to trade and competition, Sherk says. A cartel can charge higher prices only as long as it remains a monopoly. If consumers can buy elsewhere, a company must cut its prices or go out of business.

This has happened to the UAW. Nonunion workers at Honda and Toyota plants now produce high-quality cars at lower prices than are possible in Detroit. As consumers have voted with their feet, the Detroit automakers were brought to the brink of bankruptcy and begged for a bailout. The UAW has now agreed to significant concessions, eliminating some of the gap between UAW and nonunion wages.[10] With competition, union cartels break down, and unions cannot force consumers to pay higher prices or capture higher wages for their members.

Union Impact on Businesses

My wife, Angela, and I had to teach our daughters early on that money doesn't just magically appear; we have to work for it. Unions, through their practices, fail to understand that wage gains do not materialize out of thin air; they come out of business earnings. Other union policies, such as union work rules designed to increase the number of workers needed to do a job and stringent job classifications, also raise costs. Unionized companies often must raise prices to cover these costs, losing customers in the process. Fewer customers and higher costs cut business earnings, and economists find that unions have exactly this effect. Unionized companies earn lower profits than are earned by nonunion businesses.

Studies typically find that unionized companies earn profits between 10 percent and 15 percent lower than those of comparable nonunion firms, according to research in the *Review of Economics and Statistics*.[11] Unlike the findings with respect to wage effects, the research shows unambiguously that unions directly cause lower profits. Profits drop at companies whose unions win certification elections but remain at normal levels for nonunion firms. Data from the National Bureau of Economic Research found that shareholder returns fall by 10 percent over two years at companies where unions win certification.[12]

Both unions and businesses agree that unions cut profits. "They merely disagree over whether this represents a feature or a problem," Sherk said.[13]

"Unions argue that they get workers their 'fair share,' while employers complain that union contracts make them uncompetitive."

Union History

National labor unions began to form in the post–Civil War era. The Knights of Labor emerged as a major force in the late 1880s, but it collapsed because of poor organization, lack of effective leadership, disagreement over goals, and strong opposition from employers and government forces.

The American Federation of Labor, founded in 1886 and led by Samuel Gompers until his death in 1924, proved much more durable. It arose as a loose coalition of various local unions. It helped coordinate and support strikes and eventually became a major player in national politics, usually on the side of the Democrats.

American labor unions benefited greatly from the New Deal policies of Franklin Delano Roosevelt in the 1930s. The Wagner Act, in particular, legally protected the right of unions to organize. Unions from this point developed increasingly closer ties to the Democratic Party and are considered a backbone element of the New Deal coalition.

What many don't know is that the term "affirmative action" first appeared in the Wagner Act, formally known as the National Labor Relations Act. In the event of discrimination, employees were to be restored to an appropriate status in the company through "affirmative action," according to the National Labor Relations Act. While it attempted to protect workers and unions, it did not protect minorities, who were often barred from union ranks. This original coining of the term therefore has little to do with affirmative action policy as it is seen today but helped set the stage for all policy meant to compensate or address inequality.

Today, affirmative action promotes racial, ethnic, and sexual favoritism in the workplace. I still can't understand how progressive socialists can claim to be for equality of opportunity when they supports affirmative action or how they can claim to want strong businesses when they support labor unions.

Standing with Texas on Business

In contrast to progressive socialists who don't understand how labor unions impact the economy, whose taxes and wealth redistribution are impacting people in California and elsewhere so hard, Texas gets business.

Texas knows how to be inviting to business, because strong business creates the wealth that makes up a healthy society. In opposition to liberals whose support of interfering legislation chokes the life out of small business and startups, Texas works with the good ol' Western ethic to make our state hospitable. I think you can see which approach works better.

CHAPTER 8

UP BY THE BOOTSTRAPS

Social Policies That Empower the People

In the end, the difference between the conservative attitude Texas has built its history and economy on in the past and the progressive socialist attitude coming in from California and elsewhere is a difference of opinion over who knows best for the citizens of our great country. Progressive socialists believe it falls to the government to make sure its citizens are happy, successful, and secure. Conservatives know that the individual is the best determinant and defender of his or her own happiness—and that government interference will just walk on over that in the long run.

You can see this difference in conservative and progressive socialist approaches to welfare and health-care programs. Now, progressive socialists are quick to criticize conservatives for not caring about citizens. They assume that because we don't champion programs for the less fortunate, we are somehow inhumane. Listen to their rhetoric during debates and around election season. Their strategy is to corner the market on populist messaging. That's why they boldly push socialist agenda items such as guaranteed jobs and monthly stipends. It tickles itching ears.

The progressive socialists in Texas are no different than progressive socialists across the nation. When you join the side of a political party, you assume their talking points and agenda items. When I question progressive socialists in Texas, I expect them to explain the party line on specific issues. They demand that of me; I have a right to demand that of them.

Progressive socialists coming into Texas want to expand welfare. They want a single-payer health-care system. And they want to pay for both by raising the progressive income tax.

As ever, though, the programs they want to enact are shortsighted. There are a few things you might not know about welfare and health care in these United States.

Social Welfare Programs Limit the Initiative of Citizens

We have to reform the entitlement system here in America. Go back and look at the original intent of social security and consider all the different phases we've taken it through up to this point. You'll then see how we've effectively made the American people slaves to the system.

Now, I grew up in the inner city of Atlanta, Georgia. When I go back to my neighborhood, I see enslavement, not empowerment. And you don't have to go to Atlanta to see what I'm talking about; every big city in the nation has areas with clearly marked signs for victors and victims.

People come to America believing it is a land of opportunity, but if we start becoming the land of the handout, it suppresses that opportunity. If we start becoming the land of equal achievement and not equal opportunity, where the government decides how far you can go in your life, then I believe we'll lose the essence of what makes America a great nation.

Growing up in the inner city of Atlanta, Georgia, in the 1960s, I can guarantee you that my parents never would have thought that I would rise up to be a lieutenant colonel, command a battalion in combat, and become a United States congressman. I'm in awe of the fact that we live in a country where that kind of success is possible and the only thing that can hold you back is what's between your ears.

But the United States of America, land of the free, land of pioneers and trailblazers who carved out a nation with nothing more than guts and grit, has somehow become a country where we advertise for people to sign up for welfare assistance.

Lyndon B. Johnson's Great Society of domestic programs set the course for generations of government dependence. In scope, it essentially was an updated version of the New Deal domestic agenda of president Franklin D. Roosevelt in response to the Great Depression. President Johnson's main goal when he launched the programs in 1964 and 1965 was to eliminate poverty and racial injustice. It's done the exact opposite.

President Johnson's programs, coupled with president Jimmy Carter's Community Reinvestment Act of 1977, are perfect examples of shortsighted policy. The 2008 financial meltdown in the mortgage industry was directly related to Carter's policy of social engineering in the housing market under the guise of guaranteeing equality of achievement.

Under President Johnson, the federal government became more intrusive into the economy and the lives of everyday citizens. "In five years, the American government approximately doubled its regulatory role and at least doubled the scope of transfer payments," says Paul K. Conkin in his book about President Johnson, *Big Daddy from the Pedernales.*[1]

One of the programs from the Great Society was the Food Stamp Act of 1964. Its original intent was to give low-income families access to nutritional foods grown primarily by American farmers. Now, you can go on YouTube and watch a C-SPAN clip of Rep. Maxine Waters (D-CA) arguing on the House floor to permit people to use their welfare benefits in liquor stores.[2] It blows my mind.

Today, we even advertise our welfare programs to people outside of our borders. I've asked this question many times before in my speeches: Do we really want to promote the expansion of the state at the expense of our own personal sovereignty and industrialism? Are we ready to give up those freedoms? Heed the words of Benjamin Franklin: "I am for doing good to the poor, but . . . I think the best way of doing good to the poor, is not making them easy in poverty, but leading or driving them out of it. I observed . . . that the more public provisions were made for the poor, the less they provided for themselves, and of course became poorer. And, on the contrary, the less was done for them, the more they did for themselves, and became richer."[3]

And because I'm all for equal opportunity in my quotes, let's hear from Booker T. Washington in *Up from Slavery*:

> Among a large class, there seemed to be a dependence upon the government for every conceivable thing. The members of this class had little ambition to create a

position for themselves, but wanted the federal officials to create one for them. How many times I wished
then and have often wished since, that by some power
of magic, I might remove the great bulk of these people into the country districts and plant them upon the
soil, upon the solid and never deceptive foundation of
Mother Nature, where all nations and races that have
ever succeeded have gotten their start, a start that at
first may be slow and toilsome, but one that neverthe-
less is real.[4]

Progressive socialists think it's unfair that some have more than
others and that, in the name of economic fairness and social justice,
we must force people to pay their fair share. But the reality is that we
need policies that enable all to achieve prosperity and success. Welfare
should be a safety net there to catch those who may fall while climbing
the American ladder of success. The net should help them bounce
back up and continue to climb, not encourage them to lie there as if
swinging in a hammock.

In Charles Murray's 1984 classic *Losing Ground*, he said that we'd
made it "profitable for the poor to behave in the short term in ways
that were destructive in the long term." Murray goes on to say that
we've tried to "mask these long-term losses—to subsidize irretrievable
mistakes."[5]

Through our laws, we tried to provide more for the poor and instead produced more poor people. When we tried to remove the barriers to escape from poverty, we inadvertently built a trap. The Golden
State leads the nation by a long shot with $103 billion going toward

welfare. Folks, that's more than the next two on the list combined. New York comes in second, paying out $61.4 billion.[6]

Now, Texas is in third, paying out $35.4 billion, according to the US Census Bureau's Annual Surveys of State and Local Government. I'm not giving Texas a free pass, but you could make an argument that its welfare spending is more reflective of its sheer size. California can't use that argument; it's not three times larger than Texas to justify spending nearly three times more than Texas on welfare.

Welfare Fraud

Considering the mammoth welfare in the United States has grown into, it's not surprising how many individuals have found ways of beating the bloated, overcomplicated system. Every hardworking American should get enraged about stories of people scamming the system. Every time someone scams welfare, they take advantage of the hard work you did to provide for your family to trick the government into wiring your tax dollars to their bank accounts.

Illinois suspected it had a problem with welfare fraud but didn't quite know how big. The state didn't have the time or resources to check on their own. So, they hired a private contractor to identify people who might not be eligible for the low-income health program and to make recommendations for whose benefits should be canceled, according to a May 24, 2017, article from *Stateline*, a publication of the Pew Charitable Trusts.[7] Within a year, Illinois had canceled benefits for nearly 150,000 people whose eligibility could not be verified, saving the state an estimated $70 million.[8]

More states are doing the same. Mississippi enacted a law in April 2017 that will require the state to hire a private contractor to create software that reviews and checks eligibility.[9] Similar bills are being considered in Oklahoma and Ohio. Missouri and Wyoming enacted similar laws in 2016, according to *Stateline*.[10]

Fraud, overpayments, and underpayments in all assistance programs cost federal and state governments about $136.7 billion in 2015, out of about $2.8 trillion spent in assistance overall, according to a June 2016 report from the United States Government Accountability Office.[11]

On average, about 4.8 percent of assistance payments by federal and state government agencies were made in error in 2015, according to a 2016 GAO report.[12] The error rate for SNAP was estimated at about 3.7 percent and for Medicaid at about 9.8 percent.

States are particularly concerned with erroneous Medicaid payments because the program is expensive, at nearly $300 billion in 2015, and because states pay for part of it—about 37 percent in 2016.[13]

The Social Work Degree Center compiled a list of the worst cases of welfare fraud so far, and it's enough to set any true American steaming mad.[14]

- **Linda Taylor:** Nicknamed the "Welfare Queen" by the *Chicago Tribune*, Linda Taylor swindled over $150,000 each year in tax-free income from the government during the 1970s. The Illinois native used eighty different names and thirty fake home addresses to collect food stamps. She also claimed the Social Security and veterans' benefits for four deceased husbands who never existed. Linda Taylor became a notorious villain in Ronald Reagan's presidency, especially given she drove a shining Cadillac, owned four South Side homes, and frequently vacationed in Hawaii. In 1977, the forty-seven-year-old thief stood trial and was sentenced for two to six years.[15]

- **Wael Ghosheh:** Wael Ghosheh, a forty-six-year-old eatery owner from Burbank, Illinois, stole nearly $1 million in government welfare funds. The scammer fraudulently used three thousand Illinois Link cards to buy immense amounts of energy drinks and candy. He then resold the merchandise to reap big profits. Ghosheh's large-volume purchasing activity dated back over two years. One of his family members had a valid Link card that was never used. Karma caught up to Wael Ghosheh in 2015 when he was charged with five felonies, including identity theft. Yet he was released from Cook County Jail on just $50,000 bail.[16]

- **Dorothy Woods:** One of the longest criminal records for welfare fraud is held by Dorothy Mae Woods. In 1983, the enterprising Californian crook was convicted for bilking $377,000 in public aid. For a decade, Woods posed as twelve poverty-stricken women and claimed thirty-eight nonexistent children. Phony birth certificates helped her collect payments while living in a Pasadena mansion and driving a Rolls-Royce. Not learning her lesson, Dorothy Mae Woods committed fraud again in 1987. This time, she collected aid for a fourteen-year-old son who didn't live with her. In 1997,

Woods was arrested a third time for filing 135 bogus tax returns for $305,000.[17]

- **Barbara Williams:** Barbara Williams, a thirty-three-year-old woman from Los Angeles County, showed another horrific example of welfare fraud. From 1971 to 1978, Williams collected approximately $250,000 in illegal government assistance payments. She used ten different aliases to open ten separate welfare cases under the TANF program. Barbara Williams printed fake birth certificates to claim over seventy children total. She also collected around $50,000 in unwarranted food stamps. Her fraudulent funding helped her afford a luxury Ladera Heights home and four-unit apartment building. Williams even arrived at the courthouse driving a sporty silver Cadillac. In 1978, her four-day trial resulted in an eight-year prison sentence.[18]

- **Donte and Lakisha Muhammad:** The largest welfare fraud case for the Oregon Department of Human Services was perpetrated by husband-and-wife team Donte and Lakisha Muhammad. Starting in 2001, Lakisha received benefits for disabilities that left her wheelchair bound. Video was later discovered of her walking into Costco and lifting a five-gallon oilcan unassisted. Donte was paid by Oregon to serve as his wife's full-time caregiver. However, he also worked as an event planner and earned $70,000 a year. The Muhammads were caught using unjustified state payments to buy a gated Las Vegas home worth $330,000. In 2013,

Lakisha and Donte earned five-year and three-year sentences respectively.[19]

- **Andrea and Colin Chisholm III:** Colin Chisholm III, a self-proclaimed "Scottish heir," and his wife, Andrea, schemed to collect more than $167,000 in welfare payments from 2005 to 2012. The Chisholms lived near Lake Minnetonka when they began falsifying documents for public aid. Investigators eventually found the wealthy couple had hidden over $3 million in bank accounts. On taxpayers' dime, Andrea and Colin moved to Florida and bought a $1.2-million yacht. While collecting welfare from both states, the scheming duo set sail from Fort Lauderdale. The Chisholms were eventually discovered and deported from the Bahamas. In 2015, Andrea was sentenced to twelve months, and Colin was slapped with twenty-one months.[20]

- **Deborah Chisom:** Few Pennsylvania welfare fraud causes can hold a candle to Deborah Chisom's decade-long scam. From 1989 to 1999, Chisom illegally earned over $140,000 in welfare and food stamps. She claimed to be caring for her six children, who were actually living in Cleveland with her sister. Living alone, Deborah Chisom used the stolen taxpayer support to afford her drug addiction. The forty-one-year-old mother's swindle was uncovered by the state inspector after finding the children's aunt also collected welfare in Ohio. By 2000, Chisom pled guilty to welfare fraud and theft by deception. She faced a maximum fourteen-year prison sentence and $500,000 fine.

- **Fatima and Wasfi Shalhout:** Fatima and Wasfi Shalhout, a married couple from Dearborn, Michigan, committed egregious welfare fraud using their shop, Ann's Market. From 2005 to 2008, the conniving pair defrauded the Food Stamp Benefits Program for nearly $1.2 million. The Shalhouts gave customers 50 percent of their benefits in cash and pocketed the rest. For example, when beneficiaries wanted $30 in cash, they'd charge the food stamp cards $60 for phony food. Investigators found the Shalhouts used stolen funds to buy a vacation home in Israel and lease three luxury vehicles. In 2009, Wasafi was sentenced to three years, and his wife served thirty months.[21]

- **James William Smith:** Beginning in 2005, James William Smith became renowned in Minnesota as a leading voice for raising Alzheimer's awareness. In his midforties, Smith had been diagnosed with early-onset dementia and was struggling to care for two twin daughters. A local TV show declared him a "health-care hero," but this hero had a secret. James William Smith faked the medical condition by altering his speech and purposely failing memory tests. He quit his job and schemed over $6,700 each month in Social Security disability and welfare. Smith's deceit helped him afford an eighty-acre hobby farm. In 2013, he pled guilty to stealing over $144,000 in government benefits.

Cutting the fat out of the welfare programs in our nation would limit the ability for crooks like these to take advantage of your tax dollars, but the problem goes deeper than a few bad apples seeking to profit on the taxpayers' dime. The real problem is the progressive socialist idea that government welfare should make people comfortable in poverty, allowing them to abandon the American Dream to leave it.

A Push for Change

Our current social welfare programs place little to no emphasis on job training but instead focus on consumption of food, housing, and entertainment. Some states were even securing waivers from the Obama administration so that people on various welfare programs would not be required to either work or go to job training classes to keep getting benefits.

But data shows that the tide seems to be turning toward fewer benefits, thanks to conservative leadership from states like Texas. According to the USDA Food and Nutrition Service, 40 million people were using the Supplemental Nutrition Assistance Program in March 2018, down 4.6 percent from the 42 million using the program a year earlier.[22]

Republican governors and state legislators are moving ahead with proposals that would make it harder for people to get and keep welfare benefits and restrict what benefits they get, according to a January 2018 report from *Stateline*. Measures already have been floated in about a dozen states, and policy analysts say what happens in states in the coming year will serve as an indicator of what's to come nationally.[23]

Some state lawmakers are proposing new work requirements for people receiving food stamps and for people receiving government-subsidized health insurance under Medicaid. Others want welfare recipients to pass drug tests. Many are looking to crack down on fraud by requiring recipients to prove their eligibility more frequently and with better documentation. All of this could be a step in the right direction, toward encouraging a strong, motivated citizenry, empowered to solve their own problems and society instead of sitting still and giving up their rights in the hopes the government will problem solve for them.

How Single-Payer Health Care Would Limit Access to Care

Like with welfare, progressive socialists believe in government handouts for health care but fail to recognize the inherent problems in a single, nationalized program. In fact, it's become hip for our nation's intellectuals to misquote a few statistics in asserting the need for a single-payer health-care system to replace the Affordable Care Act.

After progressive socialists lost the most recent presidential election, they became more vocal in pushing for a single-payer health-care system. So far, these efforts haven't been entirely successful. In July 2017, California stopped a $400 billion proposal that its state senate passed to create a universal health-care plan for all Californians.[24] State Assembly Speaker Anthony Rendon said the lack of a funding mechanism in the bill meant the package amounted to a shell, without the ability to actually deliver the care and coverage it promises.

"There was really no there, there. It was a statement of principles, a list of values, a lot of values that I share, but it certainly wasn't a bill," Rendon told the *Hill* in July 2017. "There was absolutely no funding attached to a $400 billion proposal, no service delivery mechanism."[25]

Ideas are great until you have to pay for them. But apparently talking about costs is taboo in California. After Rendon's reasonable decision, he received death threats.

Single-payer health insurance is the ultimate government control of the health-care system. Progressive socialists cite the hopeful benefits of being able to finally avoid enrolling in health insurance every year. They say health coverage would become less expensive without the need for marketing expenses, big executive salaries, and profits. But Americans supporting single-payer health coverage don't really understand how it works.

If you get the chance to talk to doctors from countries with a single-payer system, they'll eventually get around to complaining about all of the rationing and excessive bureaucracy.

"Yet it should not surprise anyone that single-payer systems are bureaucratic and use rationing. By definition, a single-payer is a monopsony—the only purchaser of a good or service," said Devon Herrick, PhD, in a May 2017 article for *Managed Healthcare Executive*.[26]

We always hear about monopolies, where only one company has cornered the market for something that everybody wants. The federal government is quick to break that stuff up. Remember our earlier history lesson on AT&T? Well, being the only purchaser of something is equally damaging to society. If you're the only payer for a service, you get to dictate the prices you are willing to pay.

Scarce resources must always be rationed in some manner. Economic theory suggests a monopoly should set provider fees low enough that a sufficient number of providers exit the market, creating a slight shortage of services. This results in what is known as rationing by waiting. Some services or treatments may take months to receive, Herrick said.

Price controls are commonly used to limit the cost of drugs and supplies in single-payer systems like in Canada, Britain, Australia, and

New Zealand. "Doctors, medical device makers, and drug companies would all face a squeeze on fees and prices," Herrick says. "Setting hospital fees at or slightly below what Medicare pays today—about 71 percent of private insurers' fees—would significantly lower expenditures. Many single-payer health systems calculate fixed global budgets for each hospital, refusing to reimburse piecemeal for patient volume."

Rising Health-Care Costs

Now, I don't deny that the United States needs a health-care solution. The United States spends far more on health care than other high-income countries, with spending levels that rose continuously over the past three decades, according to a 2017 report from the Commonwealth Fund.[27] Even with the higher spending, however, the US population has poorer health than other countries.

On average, Americans die sooner and experience higher rates of disease and injury than people in other high-income countries, according to a report from the Institute of Medicine and National Research Council called *U.S. Health in International Perspective: Shorter Lives, Poorer Health*.[28]

The report finds that this health disadvantage exists at all ages from birth to age seventy-five and that even advantaged Americans—those who have health insurance, college educations, higher incomes, and healthy behaviors—appear to be sicker than their peers in other rich nations.

"We were struck by the gravity of these findings," says Steven H. Woolf, professor of family medicine at Virginia Commonwealth University in Richmond and chair of the panel that wrote the report. "Americans are dying and suffering at rates that we know are unnecessary because people in other high-income countries are living longer lives and enjoying better health. What concerns our panel is why, for decades, we have been slipping behind."[29]

The report looked at multiple diseases, injuries, and behaviors across the entire life span, comparing the United States with sixteen peer nations—affluent democracies that include Australia, Canada, Japan, and many Western European countries. Among these countries, the United States is at or near the bottom in nine key areas of health: infant mortality and low birth weight; injuries and homicides; teenage pregnancies and sexually transmitted infections; prevalence of HIV and AIDS; drug-related deaths; obesity and diabetes; heart disease; chronic lung disease; and disability.

Many of these health conditions disproportionately affect children and adolescents, the report says. For decades, the United States has had the highest infant mortality rate of any high-income country, and it also ranks poorly on premature birth and the proportion of children who live to age five. US adolescents have higher rates of death from traffic accidents and homicide, the highest rates of teenage pregnancy, and are more likely to acquire sexually transmitted infections. Nearly two-thirds of the difference in life expectancy between males in the United States and these other countries can be attributed to deaths before age fifty.

"It's a tragedy. Our report found that an equally large, if not larger, disadvantage exists among younger Americans," Woolf said. "I don't think most parents know that, on average, infants, children, and adolescents in the US die younger and have greater rates of illness and injury than youth in other countries."

This health disadvantage exists even though the United States spends more per capita on health care than any other nation. Although documented flaws in the health-care system may contribute to poorer health, the panel concluded that many factors are responsible for the nation's health disadvantage.

The report examines the role of underlying social values and public policies in understanding why the United States is outranked by other nations on both health outcomes and the conditions that affect health. For example, Americans are more likely to engage in certain unhealthy behaviors, from heavy caloric intake to behaviors that increase the risk of fatal injuries, the report says. The United States has relatively high rates of poverty and income inequality and is lagging behind other countries in the education of young people.

That tells me that at least some of our health problems and high death rates stem from a breakdown in the family. Feel free to disagree if you want, but my stance is rooted in the data. Suicides and drug poisonings among our young people are on the rise.[30] The post-1999 episode in midlife mortality in the United States is both historically and geographically unique, at least since 1950.[31] The turnaround is not a simple cohort effect; Americans born between 1945 and 1965 did not have particularly high mortality rates before midlife, according to research from the National Academy of Sciences of the United States of America.[32]

The three causes of death that account for the mortality reversal among white non-Hispanics are suicide, drug and alcohol poisoning (accidental and intent undetermined), and chronic liver diseases and cirrhosis.[33] All three increased year on year after 1998. We've long known about midlife increases in suicides and drug poisonings, but it's noteworthy that we've now had so many of them that it's driving up all-cause midlife mortality.

I'm not saying that a simple series of Bible studies would fix our health-care system—though it couldn't hurt—but I am saying that we've taken our emphasis off of family responsibility and replaced it with government intrusion in the way of more taxes and fanciful proposals like single-payer health care.

We need creative cost-containment solutions dovetailed with conservative values and leadership to fix our health-care system.

Timely and accessible health care could mitigate many of these challenges, but the US health-care system falls short, failing to deliver basic services reliably to all who could benefit. Overall, the United States ranks last on access to health care, according to the Commonwealth Fund's analysis. The United States has the poorest performance of all countries on affordability, scoring much lower than even the second-to-last country, Switzerland. I'd argue that calls for fiscal responsibility, best evidenced by conservatives.

Rationing Care

While a single-payer health-care system may relieve progressive in-digestion, it will leave others with extreme distress. All doctors are familiar with distortions of care associated with insurance for all paid for by some.

Have we not learned our lessons about government meddling in the private sector? In 1977, president Jimmy Carter's Community Reinvestment Act inserted the federal government into the mortgage industry. The result was the creation of toxic subprime mortgages and government-sponsored hotbeds of mismanagement such as Fannie Mae and Freddie Mac, nefarious financial practices resulting from the repeal of the Glass–Steagall Act, and, finally, a financial meltdown in

2008. Are we ready for the same impact on our health-care system as a result of making the government the sole payer?

It's one thing to take a hit to your portfolio or potentially lose your house or job because of the Great Recession. But when the US government fumbles a single-payer health-care system, get ready for a catastrophe of epic proportions.

Texas, Welfare, and Health Care

Texas isn't perfect. The state is often near or at the bottom in terms of social services, such as health care. We are the antithesis of the welfare state. And yet, we are the indisputable leader of job creation in the nation, outpacing the United States by a factor of more than two to one over two decades.[34, 35] We draw massive inflows of business investment, and we attract significant numbers of immigrants from within the United States, even more than we draw in from across the border and abroad.

Despite progressive socialist claims, more government overreach isn't the way to solve problems in the workforce and in health care. Texas-style individual independence, initiative, and fiscal conservatism will provide workable, long-term solutions—and, better yet, enable the American people to come up with solutions for themselves.

CONCLUSION

As a member of the US Army, part of what I fought for was the right for citizens to question their government when it runs afoul of its mission to its citizens. Now, finding fault with the government isn't the same thing as hating our great country. Quite the contrary; because of my love for this country, I will forever be a guardian of the republic. I follow the example of my Lord and Savior, who can both love the sinner and hate the sin. I love the state of Texas, but I hate the progressive socialism. To show the impact of progressive socialism, in this book I've rehashed some of California's failed business policies that have led to a rapid corporate exodus and discussed some of the problems with progressive socialist thinking.

All of this prose, chockful of financial data and historical business facts, is my humble campaign for your common sense. We must never let common sense be treated like a mere jacket that was once popular years ago in our youth but now no longer fits and hangs tucked away in the back of the closet.

I was taught to analyze facts and think for myself. Herman and Elizabeth Thomas West—whom I affectionately call Buck and Snooks—instilled in me a sense of faith, family, and God. They enabled me to appreciate service to our country. They taught me about fiscal responsibility, the quality of a good education, and personal responsibility. They showed me what it was like to be strong yet caring. By the time I left home to go to college, they had raised a man who would dedicate his life to being a guardian of the republic. If only more people would apply the wisdom of Buck and Snooks.

As I speak across the country, the underlying message I'm delivering is: look at the facts, and see for yourself. That's the beauty of this country; we are granted the freedom to investigate, analyze facts, and call "bovine excrement!" when something doesn't measure up.

Be like those wonderful Bereans during the first century of the church. During Paul's missionary journey, he was sent to Berea to preach about Jesus. Listen to how these Bereans reacted to Paul's teaching in Acts 17:11:

> Now the Berean Jews were of more noble character than those in Thessalonica, for they received the message with great eagerness and examined the Scriptures every day *to see if what Paul said was true.*
>
> (NIV, emphasis mine)

You also have a right to search the claims of progressive socialists "to see if what they say is true."

I started by discussing the political calculus being used to win elections for generations and generations to come. What the progressive socialist left sees in Texas is not its incredible success but rather its electoral votes. What they see is an opportunity for continuous national electoral power—power to apply policies that, as we've seen, are shortsighted and often counterproductive.

But do you know what is more damaging than political calculus? Applied mathematics. The left would alter the soul of Texas with ideological dominance. If the progressive socialist left wins Texas, they will implement policies that harken back to the same states hemorrhaging jobs.

Texas has the highest number of electoral votes among red states. And there is a possibility that Texas could gain more electoral votes due to more population coming to the Lone Star State.[1] But those that have fled left-leaning states in search of more hospitable ground may not realize why Texas is doing so darn well. And they're bringing along failed policies and ideology.

We've already spotted symptoms of their cancerous cells quickly spreading in our big cities. As city councils snatch power of attorney away from conservative people and a free market, Texas is gradually metastasizing into something unrecognizable.

The Democratic Socialists of America—the nation's largest socialist organization, with twenty-five thousand members—is growing in Austin and Houston. At the DSA's national conference in Chicago in August 2017, they elected Austin-based activist Danny Fetonte to their National Political Committee. Fetonte had gained national notoriety for helping lead the failed presidential campaign for Bernie Sanders.

Fetonte resigned from his post with the DSA after its members became aware of his involvement with the Combined Law Enforcement Associations of Texas, a powerful law enforcement union in Texas. Apparently the DSA is against law enforcement. During the same Chicago conference at which Fetonte was elected, they passed a resolution calling for the "abolition of prisons" and claimed that prisons and police were an "existential threat" to socialism and social justice movements, according to an October 13, 2017, report in the *Austin Chronicle*.[2]

But other socialist politicians are on the rise in Texas. On December 8, 2017, Austin City councilman Gregorio Casar, representing District Four in Austin, spoke at a local Democratic Socialists of America meeting to highlight the benefits of a single-payer health-care system.[3] During the speech, he unveiled plans for a local campaign to mandate paid sick leave.

During the Q&A portion of the evening's program, Casar was presented with one query from a man in the back of the room who wondered whether the second-term council member would be interested in officially joining the DSA as a card-carrying member. Put on the spot, Casar wavered for almost two beats before conceding, "I guess I should. Why not?"[4]

On Casar's city council biography, his priorities for city policy include "shared prosperity."[5] In socialist terms, that means forcibly taking from those who have and distributing to those who don't. Casar sounds an awful lot like Karl Marx. "From each according to his ability, to each according to his needs" is a slogan popularized by Marx in his 1875 *Critique of the Gotha Program*.[6]

We must ask ourselves, why the heck would any true Texan want a city councilman, of a city named after a Texas founding father, embracing the failed socialist policies of Karl Marx? I just gotta tell y'all, this Councilman Casar fella sounds stuck on stupid. Or could it be that those voting for such folly are a special kind of stupid? This reminds me of a drill sergeant saying, "Men, you can't fix stupid, but ya gotta keep it from spreading."

We have to keep the stupid from spreading throughout the Lone Star State. I'm not giving you fear-baiting "Red Scare" stuff; instead, it's a fact-based, glaring warning to Austin taxpayers.

Throughout the city of Houston, thirty-four-year-old Franklin Bynum packs campaign stops with DSA members in his bid to become a criminal court judge for the city.

"Yes, I'm running as a socialist," Mr. Bynum said in an April 20, 2018, article in the *New York Times*. "I'm a far-left candidate. What I'm trying to do is be a Democrat who actually stands for something, and tells people, 'Here's how we are going to materially improve conditions in your life.'"[7]

Rather than shy away from being called a socialist, candidates like Mr. Bynum are embracing the label. He is one of sixteen socialists who have appeared on the ballot in primary races across Texas.[8]

Since November 2016, DSA's membership has increased from about five thousand to thirty-five thousand nationwide.[9] The number of local groups has grown from 40 to 181, including 10 in Texas. Houston's once-dormant chapter now has nearly three hundred members.[10]

"We want to see money stop controlling everything. That includes politics," said Amy Zachmeyer, thirty-four, a union organizer who helped revive the Houston chapter. "That just resonates with millennials who are making less money than their parents did, are less able to buy a home, and drowning in student debt."[11]

Overall, Texas is still that beacon of hope for the nation, with longstanding conservative principles that have enabled prosperity. However, the cancer of progressive socialism is spreading.

Conservative Texans won't buckle to progressive socialists without a fight. Our steely resolve to protect hard-fought governing principles is more powerful than #Y'allidarity!

I have a stern warning for the progressive socialist left: brush up on your history before picking a fight for the soul of our state. We Texans have a legendary reputation for fighting back when provoked.

I'm reminded of when an earlier revolution caught fire. Texians, as they were called, demanded independence after Mexico denied a formal request to separate their land from the Mexican state of Coahulia.

By January of 1836, the Texian army had been fighting for three months. General Stephen Fuller Austin needed reinforcements. He ordered twenty-six-year-old Lieutenant Colonel William Barret Travis to help lead an army protecting the post of San Antonio de Béxar, which they had recently seized.

Travis encountered early problems. First, he was supposed to arrive at San Antonio de Béxar with at least one hundred men, but he arrived with only thirty volunteers. US congressman Davy Crockett and others from Tennessee joined the effort weeks later.

Second, and more crucial, Mexican president and general Antonio Lopez de Santa Anna wasn't expected to arrive at the post until mid-March. He came early. On February 23, 1836, with more than one thousand soldiers, Santa Anna had Travis's men trapped inside Misión San Antonio de Valero, also known as the Alamo.

Legend has it that Travis drew a line in the sand for his nearly two hundred defenders inside the Alamo. Crossing the line meant you were willing to fight until death. What's undisputed is that immediately after Santa Anna's surprise Alamo attack, Travis penned a

170-word letter—now housed in the Texas State Archives and Library Building in Austin, Texas—addressed to "the People of Texas & All Americans in the World." The letter and the conditions under which it was written are the stuff that makes your blood race and the hair on your forearm stand at attention.

Bejar, Feby. 24th. 1836
To the People of Texas & All Americans in the World—
Fellow Citizens & compatriots—

*I am besieged, by a thousand or more of the Mexicans under Santa Anna—I have sustained a continual Bombardment & cannonade for 24 hours & have not lost a man—The enemy has demanded a surrender at discretion, otherwise, the garrison are to be put to the sword, if the fort is taken—I have answered the demand with a cannon shot, & our flag still waves proudly from the walls—I shall never surrender or retreat. Then, I call on you in the name of Liberty, of patriotism & everything dear to the American character, to come to our aid, with all dispatch—The enemy is receiving reinforcements daily & will no doubt increase to three or four thousand in four or five days. If this call is neglected, I am determined to sustain myself as long as possible & die like a soldier who never forgets what is due to his own honor & that of his country—*Victory or Death.

William Barret Travis[12]

And yes, William Travis underlined "Victory or Death." Actually, in the original letter, he underlined it three times. With that letter, it was no longer a Texian revolution; it was now an American call to action for liberty against tyranny.

You know what happened next. After a thirteen-day siege, on March 6, 1836, Mexican troops charged the Alamo. After a ninety-minute battle of firing into darkness, Travis raced to the north wall and was killed. That moment would serve as a rallying cry for Sam Houston in a subsequent battle that sealed Texas's independence.

Today, Texas is home to more than 28.3 million people and boasts one of the world's strongest economies.[13] It's home to world-renowned universities, cutting-edge medical facilities, and an ever-growing number of Fortune 500 companies.

But more than 180 years since Travis wrote his letter, Texas once again faces a battle for liberty against tyranny. The state's ideological enemy is gaining ground. They've boasted of "turning Texas blue." Undoubtedly, if they prevail in Texas, they'll take the nation.

Our Alamo today—the conservative principles that have fostered strong economic growth—are under attack. Similar to Colonel Travis's solicitation to the United States, consider this treatise as my official request for like-minded souls to stand on guard against progressive socialism.

Texas is heralded as a success because of its low taxes and minimal regulations. We're at the top of every reputable list ranking states by business climate.[14] Even better proof that our conservative policies work are the droves of people coming into our state, namely from California, our country's standard bearer for progressive socialism.[15]

California's Conservative History

The differences between California and Texas set the stage for a national debate like no other two states in the nation. Both Texas and California have rich histories, joining the United States within five years of each other, though under different circumstances.

The Independent Republic of Texas became the twenty-eighth state in the Union on December 29, 1845. But in the wake of the 1845 annexation, Mexico still considered Texas as its northeastern province and part of its territory—even after the 1836 Texas Revolution. I suppose some lessons are harder to learn; newly elected US president James K. Polk was ready to give Mexico a reeducation.

President Polk made a proposition to the Mexican government to purchase the disputed lands between the Nueces River and the Rio Grande river further south. Mexico rejected the offer. Now offended, President Polk moved US troops further south into the disputed territory.

Mexican forces attacked an American army outpost in the occupied territory, killing twelve US soldiers and capturing fifty-two. These same Mexican troops later laid siege to an American fort along the Rio Grande. Polk cited this attack as an invasion of US territory and requested that Congress declare war. We won, of course.

Along with our win, the Alta California area—which had become part of Mexico in 1821 following its successful war for independence—was ceded to the United States. The western portion of Alta California was organized and admitted as the thirty-first state on September 9, 1850.

To California's credit, it initially followed a straighter moral compass than Texas. It pleaded to join the Union as a state that would not allow slavery. They deserve credit because they took heat from the Southern slave states for their stance. The newspaper editorials of the time reflected the will of the people. The *Californian* of March 15, 1848, says:

> We entertain several reasons why slavery should not be introduced here. First, it is wrong for it to exist anywhere. Second, not a single instance of precedence exists at present in the shape of physical bondage of our fellow men. Third, there is no excuse whatever for its introduction into this country (by virtue of climate or physical conditions). Fourth, Negroes have equal rights to life, liberty, health and happiness with the whites. Fifth, it is every individual's duty, to self and to society, to be occupied in useful employment sufficient to gain self-support. Sixth, it would be the greatest calamity that the power of the United States could inflict upon California. Seventh, we desire only a white population in California. Eighth, we left the slave states because we did not like to bring up a family in a miserable, can't-help-one's-self condition. Ninth, in conclusion we dearly love the 'Union,' but declare our positive preference for an independent condition of California to the establishment of any degree of slavery, or even the importation of free blacks.[16]

Other historians would argue that California's opposition to slavery had more to do with economic reasons than it did with any moral compass. Remember, there was gold in California. The diggers did not want the burden of digging with slaves. Of the new Californian settlers in search of gold, Walter Colton at the 1849 Constitutional Convention in Monterey said: "They know they must dig themselves; they have come out here for that purpose, and they won't degrade their calling by associating it with slave labor. Self-preservation is the first law of nature."[17]

Hear that last line? *"Self-preservation is the first law of nature."* To me, that sounds like a cornerstone conservative principle. And that's the point. Both Texan oil and Californian gold helped propel the states to great wealth. Both had a gritty self-reliance as the foundation for their success. They both started out as conservative; that's the only way they could grow.

In their own way, they were beacons guiding the United States through changes globally, economically, and culturally. California and Texas became large enough to be nation-states by themselves. Both are economic powerhouses that, combined, account for more than one-fifth of the United States' population and more than one-fifth of the country's economy.[18] That's a big deal.

You would think California would take more note of its history and pay more attention to all the companies leaving the obstructive progressive policies of their state for the conservatism of ours, but California shows little sign of changing its ways as of yet. I invite all Californians and former Californians to have a long, hard look at their policies and beliefs and just how they've been working out. Then rejoin Texas conservatives in speaking out for freedom and individual rights—or at least get out of our way in our backyard.

A New Fight

The fight against progressive socialism isn't like the fight at the Alamo. Lieutenant Colonel Travis knew he was fighting Santa Anna's Mexican troops. Unless they speak up, it's hard for us to tell from where our ideological opposition hails. However, the growing legion of progressive socialists trying to turn Texas blue could be among the thousands of Californians coming to Texas in need of a job. Oh, the irony. They could be among the growing Texas millennials—among the largest millennial populations in the nation—who increasingly support socialism over capitalism, according to the Victims of Communism poll.[19]

In either case, our fight is not against flesh and blood but against principalities and rulers of darkness, against wayward minds devoid of historical context, against unappreciative beneficiaries of shed blood enabling their freedoms, against lost prodigals too prideful to return to their first love.

But political calculus and ignorance will not be the death of us.

From the defiance at Gonzales to the immortal words of Lieutenant Colonel Travis and the courageous stand at the Alamo, to the incredible rout of Santa Anna at San Jacinto, to today's rugged individualism and entrepreneurial spirit, there is something unique about Texas. Massachusetts and Virginia may have provided America many of its Founding Fathers, but they have been overrun by an antithetical political philosophy.

Texas is a sustaining force for America, truly embodying the founding principles of America: those unalienable individual rights of life, liberty, and the pursuit of happiness.

There is, however, an ideological fight for the very soul of America and for Texas. Massachusetts and Virginia lost, but Texas will not, because in Texas it's "victory or death," and Texans dare you to "come and take it." We're keeping what we've got and extending it back to those who are lost or deluded. We advise you surrender, because we're sure not.

ACKNOWLEDGMENTS

I am a blessed fella to have had the honor to serve in uniform in the greatest nation the world has ever known and to have been the third of four generations to do so. I am truly humbled to be a Texas resident, a Tennessee Volunteer, and a son of Georgia. I want to acknowledge the highly professional and astute team at Brown Books Publishing Group, led by Milli Brown. I also want to thank Jason Roberson and acknowledge his dedication and impeccable research ability. There is no doubt that I must remember and give acknowledgment to my parents, Herman "Buck" West Sr. and Elizabeth Thomas "Snooks" West. They gave me a solid foundation, which to this day leads and guides me. As it says in Proverbs 22:6, "Train up a child in the way they should go, so that when they grow old they shall not depart from it." The way in which my parents raised me was the way of my Lord and Savior Jesus Christ, so that now I know that even though my parents have long since passed away, I have a blessed heavenly Father.

ENDNOTES

1. "Come and Take It!": A Call to Arms

1. "DSA NTX at QueerBomb," DSA North Texas, Facebook, https://www.facebook.com/events/178190709541100/.
2. "DSA North Texas Shared a Live Video," DSA North Texas, Facebook, https://www.facebook.com/DSANorthTexas/posts/64371608930 6750.
3. "June Electoral Working Group Meeting," DSA North Texas, Facebook, https://www.facebook.com/events/261655424391003/.
4. Bill Hanna, "DFW Gains a Whopping 146,000 Residents in 2017 to Lead the Nation," *Fort Worth Star-Telegram*, March 22, 2018, Fort Worth, https://www.star-telegram.com/news/local/community/fort-worth/article206357404.html ("DFW Gains 146,000 Residents").
5. Hanna, "DFW Gains 146,000 Residents."
6. "Texas Has Nation's Largest Annual State Population Growth: Births and Migration Push Population to Nearly 28 Million," Texas State Data Center, August 1, 2017, https://www.census.gov/library/stories/2017/08/texas-population-trends.html.
7. "Texas State Population Growth," Texas State Data Center.
8. W. Gardner Selby, "Greg Abbott Says If Texas Were a Country, Its Economy Would Rank 10th in World," Texas, PolitiFact, last modified September 15, 2016, http://www.politifact.com/texas/statements/2016/sep/15/greg-abbott/greg-abbott-says-if-texas-were-country-its-economy/.
9. Julieta Chiquillo, "California's Poor Flock to Texas as West Coast Homes and Jobs Fall out of Reach," *Dallas Morning News*, March 15, 2017, https://www.dallasnews.com/business/economy/2017/03/15/californias-poor-flock-texas-west-coast-homes-jobs-fall-reach.
10. Chiquillo, "California's Poor Flock to Texas."
11. Chiquillo, "California's Poor Flock to Texas."

2. Ideologies at War: Conservatism versus Progressive Socialism

1. Alexis de Tocqueville, "What Sort of Despotism Democratic Nations Have to Fear," in *Democracy in America*, trans. Henry Reeve (1899), vol. 2, bk. 4, chap. 6, http://xroads.virginia.edu/~Hyper/DETOC/ch4_06.htm.
2. Frédéric Bastiat, *The Law* (June 1850), trans. Dean Russell, Bastiat.org, accessed July 8, 2018, http://bastiat.org/en/the_law.html.
3. Bryan Burrough, *The Big Rich: The Rise and Fall of the Greatest Texas Oil Fortunes* (New York: Penguin, 2010).
4. George Norris Green, *The Establishment in Texas Politics: The Primitive Years, 1938–1957* (Westport: Greenwood Press, 1979).
5. Burrough, *The Big Rich*.
6. Kelly Miller, *Race Adjustment: The American Negro, His History and Literature* (New York: Arno Press and the *New York Times*, 1968).
7. Michael Dimock, "How America Changed during Barack Obama's Presidency," Pew Research Center, January 10, 2017, http://www.pewresearch.org/2017/01/10/how-america-changed-during-barack-obamas-presidency/.
8. Jarrett Stepman, "The Changes That Made California Become a Liberal Fiasco," *Daily Signal*, April 17, 2018, https://www.dailysignal.com/2018/04/17/the-changes-that-made-california-become-a-liberal-fiasco/.
9. Larry N. Gerston, "Top-Two Reform Tilts California toward One-Party Rule," Opinion, *Los Angeles Times*, October 5, 2016, http://www.latimes.com/opinion/op-ed/la-oe-gerston-top-two-primary-senate-race-20161005-snap-story.html.
10. Stepman, "California Liberal Fiasco."
11. Richard Fisher, "The State of the West (with Reference to George Shultz, Eisenhower, Buzz Lightyear, George Strait, the San Francisco Fed and Adam and Eve)," Federal Reserve Bank of Dallas, November 15, 2012, https://www.dallasfed.org/news/speeches/fisher/2012/fs121115.cfm.
12. Gregory Ferenstein, "The Politics of Silicon Valley," *Fast Company*, November 8, 2015, https://www.fastcompany.com/3053318/the-politics-of-silicon-valley.
13. Ferenstein, "Politics."
14. Gregory Ferenstein, "Peter Thiel's Radical Political Vision," *Daily Beast*, October 1, 2014, https://www.thedailybeast.com/peter-thiels-radical-political-vision.

15. Ferenstein, "Politics."
16. Ferenstein, "Politics."
17. Frédéric Bastiat, *That Which Is Seen, and That Which Is Not Seen* (July 1850), ed. François-René Rideau, Bastiat.org, accessed July 8, 2018, http://bastiat.org/en/twisatwins.html.
18. Ben Steverman, "This Facebook Co-Founder Wants to Tax the Rich," Bloomberg, May 4, 2018, https://www.bloomberg.com/news/features/2018-05-04/facebook-co-founder-chris-hughes-wants-universal-basic-income.
19. Steverman, "Facebook Co-Founder."
20. Steverman, "Facebook Co-Founder."
21. "Annual Report," Victims of Communism Foundation, https://www.victimsofcommunism.org/survey/.
22. "Annual Report," Victims of Communism Foundation.
23. "Annual Report," Victims of Communism Foundation.
24. Abraham Lincoln, "Address at Sanitary Fair" (speech, Baltimore, MD, April 28, 1864), in *The Collected Works of Abraham Lincoln*, ed. Roy P. Basler, vol. 7, *1863–1864* (New Brunswick: Rutgers University Press, 1953), 301–2.
25. Fisher, "The State of the West."
26. Dylan Matthews, "Cory Booker's New Big Idea: Guaranteeing Jobs for Everyone Who Wants One," Vox, April 20, 2018, https://www.vox.com/policy-and-politics/2018/4/20/17260578/cory-booker-job-guarantee-bill-full-employment-darity-hamilton.
27. Dean Baker, Sarah Rawlins, and David Stein, *The Full Employment Mandate of the Federal Reserve: Its Origins and Importance*, Center for Economic and Policy Research, Fed Up, and the Center for Popular Democracy, July 2017, Center for Economic and Policy Research, http://cepr.net/images/stories/reports/full-employment-mandate-2017-07.pdf.
28. Matthews, "Cory Booker's Big Idea."
29. Jeff Stein, "Bernie Sanders to Announce Plan to Guarantee Every American a Job," *Wonkblog* (blog), *Washington Post*, April 23, 2018, https://www.washingtonpost.com/news/wonk/wp/2018/04/23/bernie-sanders-to-unveil-plan-to-guarantee-every-american-a-job/?utm_term=.e327238a7140.
30. Stein, "Bernie Sanders to Announce Plan."

3. Texas Victorious: Success the Size of Our State

1. Kurt Badenhausen, "North Carolina Heads the Best States for Business 2017," *Forbes*, November 29, 2017, https://www.forbes.com/sites/kurtbadenhausen/2017/11/28/north-carolina-heads-the-best-states-for-business-2017/#2e3f73f9571e.
2. Badenhausen, "Best States for Business 2017."
3. Badenhausen, "Best States for Business 2017."
4. Badenhausen, "Best States for Business 2017."
5. Robert Fairlie, Arnobio Morelix, and Inara Tareque, "2017 Kauffman Index of Startup Activity: National Trends" (working paper, Kauffman Foundation, May 27, 2017, last modified June 9, 2017).
6. Dale Buss, "Best and Worst States for Business in 2018," *Chief Executive*, May 3, 2018, https://chiefexecutive.net/best-worst-states-business-2018/.
7. Buss, "Best and Worst States for Business."
8. Buss, "Best and Worst States for Business."
9. Buss, "Best and Worst States for Business."
10. W. Gardner Selby, "Greg Abbott Says If Texas Were a Country, Its Economy Would Rank 10th in World," Texas, PolitiFact, last modified September 15, 2016, http://www.politifact.com/texas/statements/2016/sep/15/greg-abbott/greg-abbott-says-if-texas-were-country-its-economy/.
11. Michael Kanellos, "HP to Acquire Compaq for $25 Billion," Tech Industry, CNET, March 10, 2002, https://www.cnet.com/news/hp-to-acquire-compaq-for-25-billion/.
12. "Texas Technology Industry Added More than 7,600 Jobs in 2017, Boosted Contribution to State's Economy," CompTIA, March 27, 2018, https://www.comptia.org/about-us/newsroom/press-releases/2018/03/27/texas-technology-industry-added-more-than-7-600-jobs-in-2017-boosted-contribution-to-state-s-economy.
13. "7,600 Jobs."
14. "7,600 Jobs."
15. "7,600 Jobs."
16. "7,600 Jobs."
17. Texas Economic Development Division, *The Texas IT Services Industry*, GO BIG in Texas, 2013, https://businessintexas.com/sites/default/files/11/13/14/it_report.pdf.
18. Texas Economic Development Division, *IT Services*.
19. Bill Hethcock, "Stream Adding to North Texas' Fast-Growing Data Center Market," Commercial Real Estate, *Dallas Business Journal*,

April 17, 2018, https://www.bizjournals.com/dallas/news/2018/04/17/stream-adding-to-north-texas-data-center-market.html.

20. Hethcock, "Stream Adding."

21. Kimberly Reeves, "Texas Film Industry Calls on Gov. Abbott to Increase Funds Set Aside for Incentives," Media & Marketing, *Austin Business Journal*, May 31, 2017, https://www.bizjournals.com/austin/news/2017/05/31/texas-film-industry-calls-on-gov-abbott-to.html.

22. Reeves, "Texas Film Industry Calls on Gov. Abbott."

23. Texas Economic Development Division, *IT Services.*

24. Texas Economic Development Division, *IT Services.*

25. Jordan Blum, "De Soto to Spindletop: How Oil Birthed Modern Houston," *Houston Chronicle*, May 22, 2016.

26. Roger M. Olien, "Oil and Gas Industry," *Handbook of Texas Online*, Texas State Historical Association, June 15, 2010, https://tshaonline.org/handbook/online/articles/doogz.

27. Bryan Burrough, *The Big Rich: The Rise and Fall of the Greatest Texas Oil Fortunes* (New York: Penguin, 2010).

28. Daniel Yergin, *The Prize: The Epic Quest for Oil, Money & Power* (New York: Simon & Schuster, 1990).

29. "Energy," GO BIG in Texas, https://businessintexas.com/industries/energy.

30. "Aerospace, Aviation & Defense," GO BIG in Texas, https://businessintexas.com/industries/aerospace-aviation-defense.

31. *Texas and the Great War Travel Guide*, Texas Historical Commission, http://www.thc.texas.gov/public/upload/publications/WWI_Texas_and_the_Great_War_TravelGuide.pdf.

32. *Texas and the Great War Travel Guide.*

33. Robert Wooster, "Military History," *Handbook of Texas Online*, Texas State Historical Association, June 15, 2010, https://tshaonline.org/handbook/online/articles/qzmtg.

34. Wooster, "Military History."

35. Forbes Corporate Communications, "Forbes Releases List of the World's Most Valuable Sports Teams," *Forbes*, July 12, 2017, https://www.forbes.com/sites/forbespr/2017/07/12/forbes-releases-list-of-the-worlds-most-valuable-sports-teams/#77886c176f5f.

36. James Barron, "Exxon Will Move Its Headquarters to Texas," Metropolitan, *New York Times*, October 27, 1989, https://www.nytimes.com/1989/10/27/nyregion/exxon-will-move-its-headquarters-to-texas.html.

37. Barron, "Exxon Will Move."

38. Barron, "Exxon Will Move."

39. ExxonMobil, *ExxonMobil 2017 Financial Statements and Supplemental Information*, https://cdn.exxonmobil.com/~/media/global/files/investor-reports/2018/2017-financial-statements.pdf.

40. ExxonMobil, *ExxonMobil 2017 Financial*.

41. "USAA 2017 Report to Members," https://usaareporttomembers.com/.

42. "USAA 2017 Report."

43. "USAA 2017 Report."

44. "USAA 2017 Report."

45. "USAA 2017 Report."

46. "USAA Company History," USAA, accessed July 08, 2018, https://www.usaa.com/inet/wc/about_usaa_corporate_overview_history.

47. Evan Hoopfer, "Exclusive: California Company Relocating to Dallas Chooses Headquarters Site," Transportation, *Dallas Business Journal*, May 17, 2018, https://www.bizjournals.com/dallas/news/2018/05/17/jetsuite-dallas-headquarter-jetsuitex.html.

48. Hoopfer, "Exclusive."

49. Hoopfer, "Exclusive."

50. Hoopfer, "Exclusive."

51. "List of Defunct Airlines in the United States," Wikimedia Foundation, last modified June 29, 2018, 22:20, https://en.wikipedia.org/wiki/List_of_defunct_airlines_of_the_United_States.

52. James P. Sterba, "Associated Press, TM New York Times," *New York Times*, November 16, 1978, https://www.nytimes.com/1978/11/16/archives/american-will-shift-headquarters-from-manhattan-to-dallas-airport.html.

53. Sterba, "Associated Press."

54. Bill Hethcock, "California Lost 9,000 Business HQs and Expansions, Mostly to Texas, 7-Year Study Says," Career and Workplace, *Dallas Business Journal*, March 22, 2018, https://www.bizjournals.com/dallas/blog/morning_call/2015/11/california-lost-9-000-business-hqs-and-expansions.html.

55. Tim Reid, "Toyota Withdrawal a Bombshell, Economic Blow to California City," Reuters, April 28, 2014, https://www.reuters.com/article/us-autos-toyota-motor-torrance/toyota-withdrawal-a-bombshell-economic-blow-to-california-city-idUSBREA3R1EW20140428.

56. Reid, "Toyota Withdrawal."

57. Bill Hethcock, "Here's the Main Reason Toyota Is Moving from California to Texas," Commercial Real Estate, *Dallas Business*

Journal, December 11, 2015, https://www.bizjournals.com/dallas/blog/2015/12/heres-the-main-reason-toyota-is-moving-from.html.

58. Hethcock, "Main Reason Toyota Is Moving."

59. Jerry Hirsch and Tim Logan, "Was Toyota Driven out of California? Not So Fast," *Los Angeles Times*, May 1, 2014, http://www.latimes.com/business/autos/la-fi-toyota-economy-20140502-story.html.

60. Bill Hethcock, "Toyota CEO Points to Plano HQ, $10B U.S. Spending, to Deflect Trump Attack," Transportation, *Dallas Business Journal*, January 9, 2017, https://www.bizjournals.com/dallas/news/2017/01/09/toyota-ceo-points-to-plano-hq-10b-u-s-spending-to.html.

61. Hethcock, "Toyota CEO."

62. Brian Womack, "AT&T Is Betting Big and Looking Westward with Time Warner," Technology, *Dallas Business Journal*, June 27, 2018, https://www.bizjournals.com/dallas/news/2018/06/27/at-t-is-betting-big-and-looking-westward-with-time.html.

63. "SW Bell to Move Headquarters to San Antonio," UPI, September 28, 1992, https://www.upi.com/Archives/1992/09/28/SW-Bell-to-move-headquarters-to-San-Antonio/4315717652800/.

64. "SW Bell to Move Headquarters."

65. "SW Bell to Move Headquarters."

66. Julie Vorman, "AT&T Closes $86 Billion BellSouth Deal," Reuters, December 30, 2006, https://www.reuters.com/article/businesspro-bellsouth-fcc-dc/att-closes-86-billion-bellsouth-deal-idUSWBT00636120061230.

67. Womack, "AT&T Betting Big."

68. Womack, "AT&T Betting Big."

69. Lori Weisberg and Jonathan Horn, "Another SD Firm Moving to Texas," *San Diego Union-Tribune*, July 18, 2014, http://www.sandiegouniontribune.com/business/economy/sdut-rick-perry-omnitracs-texas-enterprise-fund-jobs-2014jul18-story.html.

70. Weisberg and Horn, "Another SD Firm."

71. Weisberg and Horn, "Another SD Firm."

72. Weisberg and Horn, "Another SD Firm."

73. Weisberg and Horn, "Another SD Firm."

74. Weisberg and Horn, "Another SD Firm."

75. John O'Dell, "Fluor to Leave Southland for New Home in Dallas," *Los Angeles Times*, May 11, 2005, http://articles.latimes.com/2005/may/11/business/fi-fluor11.

76. O'Dell, "Fluor to Leave Southland."

77. "Annual Reports," Fluor, https://investor.fluor.com/financial-information/annual-reports.

78. O'Dell, "Fluor to Leave Southland."
79. Jacobs Engineering, "Jacobs Relocates Global Headquarters to Dallas," Jacobs, October 24, 2016, http://invest.jacobs.com/investors/Press-Release-Details/2016/Jacobs-Relocates-Global-Headquarters-to-Dallas/default.aspx.
80. Jacobs Engineering, "Jacobs Relocates."
81. Jacobs Engineering, "Jacobs Relocates."
82. Jacobs Engineering, "Jacobs Relocates."
83. Jacobs Engineering, "Jacobs Relocates."
84. "With Jacobs Engineering Move, Pasadena Must Double Down," Business, *Pasadena Star-News*, June 23, 2016, last modified August 28, 2017, https://www.pasadenastarnews.com/2016/06/23/with-jacobs-engineering-move-pasadena-must-double-down/.
85. "A History of Goodness that Dates Back to 1925," Dean Foods, http://www.deanfoods.com/our-story/brief-history/.
86. "A History of Goodness."
87. "Dean Foods Company Stock Research," NASDAQ, https://www.nasdaq.com/symbol/df/analyst-research.
88. Candace Carlisle, "California's Jamba Juice to Relocate Headquarters to Hall Office Park in Frisco," Food & Lifestyle, *Dallas Business Journal*, May 4, 2016, https://www.bizjournals.com/dallas/news/2016/05/04/californias-jamba-juice-to-relocate-headquarters.html.
89. Lindsey Juarez, "CENSUS: Frisco Ranks as No. 1 Fastest-Growing U.S. City," *Community Impact Newspaper*, May 23, 2018, https://communityimpact.com/dallas-fort-worth/frisco/city-county/2018/05/23/census-frisco-ranks-as-no-1-fastest-growing-u-s-city/.
90. Carlisle, "California's Jamba Juice to Relocate."
91. Frisco Economic Development Corporation, "FRISCO: City Receives Highest Bond Rating Possible for First Time in City's History; Translates Into Lower Interest Rates, 'Strong Fiscal Position,'" FriscoEDC.com, June 1, 2018, http://friscoedc.com/news/frisco-city-receives-highest-bond-rating-possible-first-time-citys-history-translates-lower.
92. Frisco Economic Development Corporation, "FRISCO."
93. Frisco Economic Development Corporation, "FRISCO."
94. Rob Arias, "City of Emeryville Facing 1.2M Budget Shortfall with Bleaker Future Projections. Cuts & New Taxes Looming?," *E'ville Eye*, June 9, 2017, https://evilleeye.com/news-commentary/city-of-emeryville-facing-1-2-mm-budget-shortfall-with-bleaker-projections-cuts-new-taxes-looming/.

95. Arias, "City of Emeryville Facing Shortfall."
96. Arias, "City of Emeryville Facing Shortfall."
97. Arias, "City of Emeryville Facing Shortfall."
98. Arias, "City of Emeryville Facing Shortfall."
99. Arias, "City of Emeryville Facing Shortfall."
100. Arias, "City of Emeryville Facing Shortfall."
101. Darwin BondGraham, "Key Measures Are on June Ballot," *East Bay Express*, May 16, 2018, https://www.eastbayexpress.com/oakland/IssueArchives?issue=16110414.

4. The Decline of Liberalism: Why California Is Always a Seller's Market

1. Brian Uhler and Justin Garosi, "California Losing Residents via Domestic Migration," Legislative Analyst's Office, the California Legislature's Nonpartisan Fiscal and Policy Advisor, February 21, 2018, https://lao.ca.gov/LAOEconTax/Article/Detail/265.
2. Mac Taylor, *California's High Housing Costs: Causes and Consequences*, Legislative Analyst's Office, the California Legislature's Nonpartisan Fiscal and Policy Advisor, March 17, 2015, http://www.lao.ca.gov/reports/2015/finance/housing-costs/housing-costs.aspx.
3. Taylor, *California's High Housing Costs*.
4. Arin Greenwood, "The Median Home Price Is $188,900. Here's What That Actually Buys You," *HuffPost*, March 13, 2014, Home & Living, https://www.huffingtonpost.com/2014/03/13/median-home-price-2014_n_4957604.html.
5. Taylor, *California's High Housing Costs*.
6. Taylor, *California's High Housing Costs*.
7. Taylor, *California's High Housing Costs*.
8. Taylor, *California's High Housing Costs*.
9. Taylor, *California's High Housing Costs*.
10. Taylor, *California's High Housing Costs*.
11. Taylor, *California's High Housing Costs*.
12. Taylor, *California's High Housing Costs*.
13. Taylor, *California's High Housing Costs*.
14. Taylor, *California's High Housing Costs*.
15. Taylor, *California's High Housing Costs*.

16. Henry Grabar, "These Graphs Explain Why California's Property-Tax Regime Is the Worst," *Moneybox* (blog), *Slate*, September 22, 2016, http://www.slate.com/blogs/moneybox/2016/09/22/california_s_proposition_13_is_bad_policy_and_here_are_some_graphs_to_show.html.

17. Taylor, *California's High Housing Costs*.

18. Grabar, "California's Property-Tax Regime."

19. Grabar, "California's Property-Tax Regime."

20. Jennifer Hernandez, "California Environmental Quality Act Lawsuits and California's Housing Crisis," *Hastings Environmental Law Journal* 24, no. 1 (Winter 2018): 20–71, 2018. http://journals.uchastings.edu/journals/websites/west-northwest/HELJ_V_24_1.pdf.

21. Hernandez, "California Environmental Quality Act Lawsuits."

22. Chang-Tai Hsieh and Enrico Moretti, "How Local Housing Regulations Smother the U.S. Economy," Opinion, *New York Times*, September 6, 2017, https://www.nytimes.com/2017/09/06/opinion/housing-regulations-us-economy.html.

23. Corey Protin, Matthew Stuart, and Matt Weinberger, "Animated Timeline Shows How Silicon Valley Became a $2.8 Trillion Neighborhood," *Business Insider*, May 30, 2017, http://www.businessinsider.com/silicon-valley-history-technology-industry-animated-timeline-video-2017-5.

24. Noam Cohen, *The Know-It-Alls: The Rise of Silicon Valley as a Political Powerhouse and Social Wrecking Ball* (New York: New Press, 2017).

25. Mallory Locklear, "Google Gets Closer to Building Its Own City in San Jose," *Engadget* (blog), June 21, 2017, https://www.engadget.com/2017/06/21/google-closer-building-city-san-jose/.

26. "What Is in the Republicans' Final Tax Bill," Reuters, December 13, 2017, https://www.reuters.com/article/us-usa-tax-changes-factbox/what-is-in-the-republicans-final-tax-bill-idUSKBN1E8030.

27. Marc Stiles, "Seattle City Council Approves Head Tax to Raise $237 million for Homeless Services and Housing," Government & Regulations, *Puget Sound Business Journal*, May 14, 2018, https://www.bizjournals.com/seattle/news/2018/05/14/seattle-city-council-approves-head-tax-amazon.html.

28. Stiles, "Seattle City Council Approves Head Tax."

29. Stiles, "Seattle City Council Approves Head Tax."

30. Eric Newcomer, "Silicon Valley Cities, San Francisco Look at a Head Tax Like Seattle's," *Seattle Times*, May 23, 2018, https://

www.seattletimes.com/business/technology/silicon-valley
-cities-san-francisco-look-at-a-head-tax-like-seattle/.

31. Bill Hethcock, "Expert: Proposed Corporate Tax Hike in California Could Drive More Businesses to Texas," Government & Regulations, *Dallas Business Journal*, March 20, 2018, https://www. bizjournals.com/dallas/news/2018/03/20/expert-proposed-corpo-rate-tax-hike-in-california.html.

5. The Friendly State: A Tax Code That Pays

1. Tax Foundation, *Tax Freedom Day 2018 is April 19th*, https://files. taxfoundation.org/20180411105322/Tax-Foundation-TFD-2018. pdf.
2. Tax Foundation, *Tax Freedom Day*.
3. "Taxes in Texas," Tax Foundation, https://taxfoundation.org/state/ texas/.
4. "Taxes in Texas."
5. "Taxes in Texas."
6. "Taxes in Texas."
7. "Taxes in Texas."
8. "Taxes in Texas."
9. Kyle Pomerleau, *Understanding the Marriage Penalty and Marriage Bonus*, Tax Foundation, April 23, 2015, https://files.taxfoundation. org/legacy/docs/TaxFoundation_FF464.pdf.
10. Pomerleau, *Understanding the Marriage Penalty*.
11. Jason J. Fichtner and Jacob Feldman, *The Hidden Costs of Tax Compliance*, Mercatus Center at George Mason University, May 20, 2013, Federal Fiscal Policy, https://www.mercatus.org/publication/ hidden-costs-tax-compliance.
12. "NSA Survey Reveals Fee and Expense Data for Accounting Firms in 2016 and 2017 Projections," *NSA Blogger* (blog), National Society of Accountants Member Connect, January 27, 2017, https://connect. nsacct.org/blogs/nsa-blogger/2017/01/27/nsa-survey-reveals-fee-and-expense-data-for-tax-accounting-firms-in-2016-and-2017-projections.
13. "NSA Survey Reveals."
14. "NSA Survey Reveals."

15. "NSA Survey Reveals."
16. "NSA Survey Reveals."
17. Scott A. Hodge, "The Compliance Costs of IRS Regulations," Fiscal Fact no. 512, Tax Foundation, June 15, 2016, https://taxfoundation.org/compliance-costs-irs-regulations/.
18. Hodge, "Compliance Costs."
19. Hodge, "Compliance Costs."
20. "Why Are Taxes So Complicated?," Tax Policy Center's Briefing Book, Tax Policy Center, https://www.taxpolicycenter.org/briefing-book/why-are-taxes-so-complicated.
21. "2018 and Prior Year Filing Statistics," IRS, last modified July 13, 2018, https://www.irs.gov/newsroom/2018-and-prior-year-filing-season-statistics.
22. Kay Bell, "Getting IRS Tax Help Gets a Bit More Complicated," *Don't Mess with Taxes: Translating Taxes into Money-Saving English* (blog), February 15, 2018, http://www.dontmesswithtaxes.com/2018/02/getting-irs-tax-help-gets-a-bit-more-complicated.html.
23. "Examples of Abusive Tax Schemes–Fiscal Year 2017," IRS, last modified February 17, 2018, https://www.irs.gov/compliance/criminal-investigation/examples-of-abusive-tax-schemes-fiscal-year-2017.
24. "Abusive Tax Schemes."
25. "Abusive Tax Schemes."
26. Chris Edwards and Vanessa Brown Calder, "Low-Income Housing Tax Credit: Costly, Complex, and Corruption-Prone," Cato Institute, Tax and Budget Bulletin no. 17, November 13, 2017, https://www.cato.org/publications/tax-budget-bulletin/low-income-housing-tax-credit-costly-complex-corruption-prone.
27. Edwards and Calder, "Low-Income Housing Tax Credit."
28. Kyle Pomerleau, Jared Walczak, and Scott A. Hodge, *2017 International Tax Competitiveness Index*, Tax Foundation, October 31, 2017, https://taxfoundation.org/2017-international-tax-competitiveness-index/.
29. Pomerleau, Walczak, and Hodge, *2017 Tax Competitiveness*.
30. Pomerleau, Walczak, and Hodge, *2017 Tax Competitiveness*.
31. "Scam Alert: IRS Urges Taxpayers to Watch Out for Erroneous Refunds; Beware of Fake Calls to Return Money to a Collection Agency," IRS, February 13, 2018, https://www.irs.gov/newsroom/scam-alert-irs-urges-taxpayers-to-watch-out-for-erroneous-refunds-beware-of-fake-calls-to-return-money-to-a-collection-agency.

6. Live and Let Live: Minimal Regulation

1. National Small Business Association, "New Survey: Regulations a Major Issue for Small Business," news release, January 17, 2017, http://nsba.biz/new-survey-regulations-a-major-issue-for-small-business/.

2. "2017 Small Business Profiles for the States and Territories," US Small Business Administration, https://www.sba.gov/advocacy/2017-small-business-profiles-states-and-territories.

3. National Small Business Association, "New Survey."

4. National Small Business Association, "New Survey."

5. Wayne Winegarden, *The 50-State Small Business Regulation Index* (San Francisco: Pacific Research Institute, 2015).

6. "2017 Small Business Profiles."

7. Winegarden, *50-State Regulation Index*.

8. Winegarden, *50-State Regulation Index*.

9. "Form 10-K—D.R. Horton," SEC.gov, November 15, 2017, https://www.sec.gov/Archives/edgar/data/882184/000088218417000103/a2017930-10k.htm.

10. "Form 10-K."

11. "D. R. Horton, Inc. History," Funding Universe, http://www.funding-universe.com/company-histories/d-r-horton-inc-history/.

12. "D. R. Horton History."

13. Mitchell Schnurman, "How D.R. Horton Is Boosting Its Dominance," *D CEO*, March 2011, https://www.dmagazine.com/publications/d-ceo/2011/march/how-homebuilder-dr-horton-is-boosting-its-dominance/.

14. Candace Carlisle, "D.R. Horton Ups the Ante to Land Forestar in Key Acquisition Deal," Residential, *Dallas Business Journal*, June 23, 2017, https://www.bizjournals.com/dallas/news/2017/06/23/d-r-horton-ups-the-ante-to-land-forestar-in-key.html.

15. Winegarden, *50-State Regulation Index*.

16. Joseph Nixon and the Texas Public Policy Foundation, *Ten Years of Tort Reform in Texas: A Review*, Heritage Foundation, July 26, 2013, https://www.heritage.org/report/ten-years-tort-reform-texas-review.

17. Nixon and the Texas Public Policy Foundation, *Ten Years*.

18. Nixon and the Texas Public Policy Foundation, *Ten Years*.

19. Robert Henneke and James Quintero, "Commentary: Austin Tree Ordinance Violates Private Property Rights," Opinion, *Austin American-Statesman*, March 25, 2017, https://www.mystatesman.com/news/opinion/commentary-austin-tree-ordinance-violates-private-property-rights/yyQXJGm9tJcPlcQet8sNJN/.

20. "Detailed Code Violations," City of College Station, http://www.
    cstx.gov/index.aspx?page=513.
21. Aleem Maqbool, "The Texas Town that Banned Fracking (and
    Lost)," BBC News, June 16, 2015, https://www.bbc.com/news/
    world-us-canada-33140732.
22. Hei Sing (Ron) Chan, Shanjun Li, and Fan Zhang, "Firm
    Competitiveness and the European Union Emissions Trading
    Scheme," *Energy Policy* 63 (December 2013): 1056–64, https://www.
    sciencedirect.com/science/article/pii/S0301421513009567?via
    =ihub.
23. Chan, Li, and Zhang, "Firm Competitiveness."
24. Carl Pasurka, "Perspectives on Pollution Abatement and Compet-
    itiveness: Theory, Data, and Analyses," *Review of Environmental
    Economics Policy* 2, no. 2 (July 24, 2008): 194–218, https://doi.org/
    10.1093/reep/ren009.
25. Pasurka, "Perspectives."
26. Cary Coglianese, Adam M. Finkel, and Christopher Carrigan, *Does
    Regulation Kill Jobs?* (Philadelphia: University of Pennsylvania
    Press, 2015).
27. Michael E. Porter and Claas van der Linde, "Toward a New
    Conception of the Environment-Competitiveness Relationship,"
    Journal of Economic Perspectives 9, no. 4 (1995): 97–118.
28. Gary D. Libecap, "The High Price of Environmental Regulations,"
    Defining Ideas, Hoover Institution, June 25, 2015, https://www.
    hoover.org/research/high-price-environmental-regulations.
29. Libecap, "High Price of Environmental Regulations."
30. Libecap, "High Price of Environmental Regulations."
31. Libecap, "High Price of Environmental Regulations."
32. Libecap, "High Price of Environmental Regulations."
33. Barack Obama, "Letter from the President—Arctic National
    Refuge Proposed Designations," news release, Obama White House
    Archives, April 3, 2015, https://obamawhitehouse.archives.gov/
    the-press-office/2015/04/03/letter-president-arctic-national-wild-
    life-refuge-proposed-designations.
34. "President Obama Protects a Valued Wilderness," Editorial, *New York
    Times*, January 27, 2015, https://www.nytimes.com/2015/01/27/
    opinion/president-obama-protects-a-valued-wilderness.html.
35. Capital Area Council of Governments Air Program, *The Potential
    Costs of an Ozone Nonattainment Designation to Central Texas*,
    Capital Area Council of Governments, September 22, 2015, http://
    www.capcog.org/documents/airquality/reports/2015/Potential_
    Costs_of_a_Nonattainment_Designation_09-17-15.pdf.

36. CAPCOG Air Program, *Potential Costs.*
37. CAPCOG Air Program, *Potential Costs.*
38. CAPCOG Air Program, *Potential Costs.*
39. CAPCOG Air Program, *Potential Costs.*
40. CAPCOG Air Program, *Potential Costs.*
41. CAPCOG Air Program, *Potential Costs.*
42. CAPCOG Air Program, *Potential Costs.*
43. CAPCOG Air Program, *Potential Costs.*
44. CAPCOG Air Program, *Potential Costs.*
45. CAPCOG Air Program, *Potential Costs.*
46. Small Business Committee, "Occupational Hazards: How Excessive Licensing Hurts Small Business," news release, February 27, 2018, https://smallbusiness.house.gov/news/documentsingle.aspx?DocumentID=400648.
47. Small Business Committee, "Occupational Hazards."
48. Kurt Erickson, "Missouri Set to Ease Regulations on Hair Braiders," Political Fix, *St. Louis Post-Dispatch*, May 1, 2018, https://www.stltoday.com/news/local/govt-and-politics/missouri-set-to-ease-regulations-on-hair-braiders/article_7010782a-975e-5a92-bb18-c34107399c87.html.
49. Erickson, "Missouri Set to Ease Regulations."
50. Small Business Committee, "Occupational Hazards."
51. Small Business Committee, "Occupational Hazards."
52. Small Business Committee, "Occupational Hazards."
53. Small Business Committee, "Occupational Hazards."
54. Small Business Committee, "Occupational Hazards."
55. "Department of Labor Fiduciary Rule," American Bankers Association, https://www.aba.com/Advocacy/Issues/Pages/DOL-Fiduciary-Rule.aspx.
56. "The DOL Fiduciary Rule Explained," Investopedia, June 25, 2018, https://www.investopedia.com/updates/dol-fiduciary-rule/.
57. "FACT SHEET: Middle Class Economics: Strengthening Retirement Security by Cracking Down on Backdoor Payments and Hidden Fees," Obama White House Archives, February 23, 2015, https://obamawhitehouse.archives.gov/the-press-office/2015/02/23/fact-sheet-middle-class-economics-strengthening-retirement-security-crac.
58. "What You Should Know about EEOC's Proposal to Collect Pay Data," US Equal Employment Opportunity Commission, https://www.eeoc.gov/eeoc/newsroom/wysk/proposal_pay_data.cfm.

59. Danielle Paquette, "The Trump Administration Just Halted this Obama-Era Rule to Shrink the Gender Wage Gap," *Wonkblog* (blog), *Washington Post*, August 30, 2017, https://www.washingtonpost.com/news/wonk/wp/2017/08/30/the-trump-administration-just-halted-this-obama-era-rule-to-shrink-the-gender-wage-gap/?utm_term=.292a9586807c.

60. "What You Should Know."

61. Randel K. Johnson and James Plunkett, letter to John M. Mulvaney, February 27, 2017, Chamber of Commerce of the United States of America, https://www.uschamber.com/sites/default/files/2-27-17_comment_letter_-_us_chamber_eeo-1_request_for_review.pdf.

62. Johnson and Plunkett to Mulvaney.

63. Paquette, "Trump Administration Just Halted Rule to Shrink Gender Wage Gap."

64. Celine McNicholas and Marni von Wilpert, *The Joint Employer Standard and the National Labor Relations Board: What Is at Stake for Workers?*, Economic Policy Institute, May 31, 2017, https://www.epi.org/publication/the-joint-employer-standard-and-the-national-labor-relations-board-what-is-at-stake-for-workers/.

65. "FAQ: Joint Employer Standard," Competitive Enterprise Institute, https://cei.org/content/faq-joint-employer-standard.

66. "FAQ: Joint Employer Standard."

67. "FAQ: Joint Employer Standard."

68. "FAQ: Joint Employer Standard."

69. "FAQ: Joint Employer Standard."

70. McNicholas and von Wilpert, *What Is at Stake for Workers?*

71. McNicholas and von Wilpert, *What Is at Stake for Workers?*

72. McNicholas and von Wilpert, *What Is at Stake for Workers?*

73. "Misclassification of Employees as Independent Contractors," Department for Professional Employees, http://dpeaflcio.org/programs-publications/issue-fact-sheets/misclassification-of-employees-as-independent-contractors/.

74. "Misclassification of Employees."

75. "Misclassification of Employees."

76. "Misclassification of Employees."

77. "Misclassification of Employees."

78. "Misclassification of Employees."

79. "Fact Sheet: Final Rule to Update the Regulations Defining and Delimiting the Exemption for Executive, Administrative, and Professional Employees," Wage and Hour Division, United States Department of Labor, May 2016, https://www.dol.gov/whd/overtime/final2016/overtime-factsheet.htm.

80. "Fact Sheet: Final Rule."
81. Job Creators Network, *Testimony of Adam Robinson, CEO and Co-Founder, Hireology, Member of the Job Creators Network, before the Small Business Committee, U.S. House of Representatives: How the Department of Labor Overtime Rule Impacts Technology Startups and High-Growth Small Businesses, June 23, 2016*, Small Business Committee, https://smallbusiness.house.gov/uploaded-files/6-23-16_robinson_testimony.pdf.
82. Chris Opfer, "Texas Judge Kills Obama Overtime Rule," News, Bloomberg, August 31, 2017, https://www.bna.com/texas-judge-kills-n73014463988/.

7. Southern Hospitality: Probusiness Policies

1. "Texas Enterprise Fund (TEF) as of June 30, 2018," Office of the Governor, https://gov.texas.gov/uploads/files/business/TEF_Listing_6-30-2018.pdf.
2. "Texas Enterprise Fund 2018."
3. Richard Vedder, *Ohio Right-to-Work: How the Economic Freedom of Workers Enhances Prosperity*, Buckeye Institute for Public Policy Solutions, March 1, 2012, https://www.heartland.org/publications-resources/publications/ohio-right-to-work-how-the-economic-freedom-of-workers-enhances-prosperity?source=policybot.
4. Franklin D. Roosevelt, "101–Statement on Signing the National Labor Relations Act.," July 5, 1935, American Presidency Project, http://www.presidency.ucsb.edu/ws/?pid=14893.
5. Michael Pierce, "Vance Muse and the Racist Origins of Right-to-Work," *ACSblog*, American Constitution Society, February 20, 2018, https://www.acslaw.org/acsblog/vance-muse-and-the-racist-origins-of-right-to-work.
6. James Sherk, "What Unions Do: How Labor Unions Affect Jobs and the Economy," Heritage Foundation, May 21, 2009, Jobs and Labor, https://www.heritage.org/jobs-and-labor/report/what-unions-do-how-labor-unions-affect-jobs-and-the-economy.
7. Sherk, "What Unions Do."
8. Sherk, "What Unions Do."
9. Sherk, "What Unions Do."

10. Bill Vlasic, "Union Makes Concessions to Help Automakers," *New York Times*, December 3, 2008, Business Day, https://www.nytimes.com/2008/12/04/business/04auto.html.

11. Barry T. Hirsch, "Union Coverage and Profitability among U.S. Firms," *Review of Economics and Statistics* 73, no. 1 (February 1991): 69–77, https://www.jstor.org/stable/2109688?seq=1#page_scan_tab_contents.

12. Hirsch, "Union Coverage and Profitability."

13. Sherk, "What Unions Do."

8. Up by the Bootstraps: Social Policies

That Empower the People

1. Paul K. Conkin, *Big Daddy from the Pedernales* (Woodbridge: Twayne Press, 1987).

2. "Maxine Waters Wants Welfare for Winos," YouTube video, 4:24, posted by "ReidBaerPoetry," February 1, 2012, https://www.youtube.com/watch?v=WUzOCtdiyrk.

3. "Quote by Benjamin Franklin," Goodreads, accessed July 9, 2018, https://www.goodreads.com/quotes/23892-i-am-for-doing-good-to-the-poor-but-i-think.

4. Booker T. Washington, *Up from Slavery: An Autobiography* (Garden City: Doubleday, 1901; University Library, University of North Carolina at Chapel Hill, 1997), 90, https://docsouth.unc.edu/fpn/washington/washing.html.

5. Charles A. Murray, *Losing Ground: American Social Policy, 1950–1980* (New York: BasicBooks, 1984), 9.

6. Shawn Langlois, "No Other State Comes Close to California in Terms of Total Welfare Spending," MarketWatch, November 28, 2017, https://www.marketwatch.com/story/no-other-state-comes-close-to-california-when-it-comes-to-welfare-spending-2017-11-28.

7. Jen Fifield, "What Happens When States Go Hunting for Welfare Fraud," *Stateline* (blog), Pew, May 24, 2017, http://www.pewtrusts.org/en/research-and-analysis/blogs/stateline/2017/05/24/what-happens-when-states-go-hunting-for-welfare-fraud.

8. Fifield, "When States Go Hunting for Welfare Fraud."

9. Fifield, "When States Go Hunting for Welfare Fraud."

10. Fifield, "When States Go Hunting for Welfare Fraud."

11. Government Accountability Office, *Improper Payments: CFO Act Agencies Need to Improve Efforts to Address Compliance Issues*, Government Accountability Office Report to Congressional Committees, June 2016, https://www.gao.gov/assets/680/678154.pdf.

12. GAO, *Improper Payments*.

13. GAO, *Improper Payments*.

14. "10 Worst Cases of Welfare Fraud Ever (So Far)," Social Work Degree Center, https://www.socialworkdegreecenter.com/10-worst -cases-welfare-fraud-ever-far/.

15. Josh Levin, "The Welfare Queen," *Slate*, December 19, 2013, http:// www.slate.com/articles/news_and_politics/history/2013/12/ linda_taylor_welfare_queen_ronald_reagan_made_her_a_notori- ous_american_villain.html.

16. Rosemary Sobol, "Prosecutors: 3,000 LINK Cards Used to Buy 'Massive Amounts' of Candy, Energy Drinks," *Chicago Tribune*, March 13, 2015, http://www.chicagotribune.com/news/local/ breaking/chi-link-card-million-dollar-scam20150313-story.html.

17. Lois Timnick, "'Welfare Queen' Arrested on New Fraud Charges," *Los Angeles Times*, May 22, 1987, http://articles.latimes.com/1987 -05-22/news/mn-1219_1_welfare-fraud.

18. "8 Years for Huge Fraud Case," *Milwaukee Sentinel*, December 29, 1978, Google News Archive, https://news.google.com/news- papers?nid=1368&dat=19781229&id=woRQAAAAIBAJ&sjid =-RIEAAAAIBAJ&pg=1834,6718862&hl=en.

19. Rick Bella, "Nevada Couple Sentenced in Oregon's Largest Case of Welfare Fraud," *Oregonian*, May 16, 2013, https://www.oregonlive. com/clackamascounty/index.ssf/2013/05/post_104.html.

20. Brittany Shammas, "'Scottish Aristocrat' Sentenced 21 Months in Prison for Welfare Fraud," *Sun-Sentinel*, January 5, 2015, http:// www.sun-sentinel.com/local/palm-beach/fl-colin-chisholm-sen- tencing-20150105-story.html.

21. Chad Halcom, "Store President, Manager Sentenced to Prison for Fraud," *Crain's Detroit Business*, May 5, 2009, last modified March 15, 2017, http://www.crainsdetroit.com/article/20090505/ FREE/905059957/store-president-manager-sentenced-to-prison -for-fraud.

22. "Data and Statistics," Food and Nutrition Service, United States Department of Agriculture, https://www.fns.usda.gov/ data-and-statistics.

23. "State of the States 2018," *Stateline* (blog), Pew, January 22, 2018, http://www.pewtrusts.org/en/research-and-analysis/blogs/stateline/2018/01/22/state-of-the-states-2018.

24. Reid Wilson, "Battle Breaks Out in California over Single-Payer Healthcare," *Hill*, July 2, 2017, http://thehill.com/homenews/state-watch/340319-battle-breaks-out-in-california-over-single-payer-healthcare.

25. Wilson, "Battle Breaks Out."

26. Devon Herrick, "Opinion: Biggest Problems with Single-Payer 'Medicare-for-All,'" Managed Healthcare Executive, May 21, 2017, http://www.managedhealthcareexecutive.com/business-strategy/opinion-biggest-problems-single-payer-medicare-all.

27. Eric C. Schneider et al., *Mirror, Mirror 2017: International Comparison Reflects Flaws and Opportunities for Better U.S. Health Care*, Commonwealth Fund, July 14, 2017, https://www.commonwealthfund.org/publications/fund-reports/2017/jul/mirror-mirror-2017-international-comparison-reflects-flaws-and.

28. Institute of Medicine and National Research Council, *U.S. Health in International Perspective: Shorter Lives, Poorer Health* (Washington, DC: National Academies Press, 2013).

29. Institute of Medicine and National Research Council, *U.S. Health*.

30. Institute of Medicine and National Research Council, *U.S. Health*.

31. Institute of Medicine and National Research Council, *U.S. Health*.

32. Institute of Medicine and National Research Council, *U.S. Health*.

33. Institute of Medicine and National Research Council, *U.S. Health*.

34. Vance Ginn, "Texas Leads in Job Creation," news release, Texas Public Policy Foundation, May 18, 2018, https://www.texaspolicy.com/press_release/detail/texas-leads-in-jobs-creation.

35. Chuck DeVore, "Texas Laps California in Job and Population Growth," *Forbes*, May 22, 2018, https://www.forbes.com/sites/chuckdevore/2018/05/22/texas-laps-california-in-job-and-population-growth/#51ae1b9c73f3.

Conclusion

1. Jeremy Wallace, "Texas Expected to Get More Clout in Future Presidential Contests," *Houston Chronicle*, December 27, 2017, https://www.chron.com/news/politics/texas/article/Texas-about-to-get-even-bigger-in-presidential-12455940.php.

2. Mary Tuma, "Learning the Hard Way that Police and Democratic Socialists Rarely Mix," News, *Austin Chronicle*, October 13, 2017, https://www.austinchronicle.com/news/2017-10-13/learning-the-hard-way-that-police-and-democratic-socialists-rarely-mix/.

3. "Reporter's Notebook: Why Not?" *Austin Monitor*, December 11, 2017, https://www.austinmonitor.com/stories/2017/12/reporters-notebook-not/.

4. "Reporter's Notebook."

5. Farah Stockman, "'Yes, I'm Running as a Socialist.' Why Candidates Are Embracing the Label in 2018," *New York Times*, April 20, 2018, https://www.nytimes.com/2018/04/20/us/dsa-socialism-candidates-midterms.html.

6. Karl Marx, *Critique of the Gotha Program* (first published 1890–91), Marxists.org, https://www.marxists.org/archive/marx/works/1875/gotha/.

7. Stockman, "Running as a Socialist."

8. Stockman, "Running as a Socialist."

9. Stockman, "Running as a Socialist."

10. Stockman, "Running as a Socialist."

11. Stockman, "Running as a Socialist."

12. William Barret Travis to the People of Texas & All Americans in the World, February 24, 1836, "The Letter," The Travis Letter Returns, http://www.travisletter.com/the-letter.html.

13. "Texas Population," World Population Review, January 23, 2018, http://worldpopulationreview.com/states/texas-population/.

14. "America's Top States for Business 2018," CNBC, July 10, 2018, https://www.cnbc.com/2018/07/10/americas-top-states-for-business-2018.html.

15. Chuck DeVore, "Texas Laps California in Job and Population Growth," *Forbes*, May 22, 2018, https://www.forbes.com/sites/chuckdevore/2018/05/22/texas-laps-california-in-job-and-population-growth/#51ae1b9c73f3.

16. "Slavery in California," *Californian*, March 15, 1848, California Digital Newspaper Collection, https://cdnc.ucr.edu/cgi-bin/cdnc?a=d&d=C18480315.2.3.

17. Kevin Howe, "State Constitutional Convention Re-created in Monterey," *Monterey Herald*, October 10, 2011, http://www.montereyherald.com/article/zz/20111010/NEWS/111018766.
18. "U.S. States Comparison: Texas vs California," CountryEconomy.com, https://countryeconomy.com/countries/usa-states/compare/texas/california.
19. "Annual Report," Victims of Communism Foundation, https://www.victimsofcommunism.org/survey/.

ABOUT THE AUTHOR

Allen Bernard West is the third of four generations of military service-men in his family. During his twenty-two-year career in the United States Army, Lieutenant Colonel West served in several combat zones and received many honors, including a Bronze Star, three Meritorious Service Medals, three Army Commendation Medals—one with Valor device, and a Valorous Unit Award. In November of 2010, West was elected to the United States Congress, representing Florida's Twenty-Second District. As a member of the 112th Congress, he sat on the Small Business and Armed Services Committees and was instrumental in the passage of the 2011 and 2012 National Defense Authorization Acts.

Lt. Col. West is a Fox News contributor, director of the Booker T. Washington Initiative at the Texas Public Policy Foundation, senior fellow at the Media Research Center, contributing columnist for Townhall.com, and author of *Guardian of the Republic: An American Ronin's Journey to Family, Faith and Freedom.*

Lt. Col. West is the former executive director of the National Center for Policy Analysis in Dallas, Texas; a legacy life member of the Veterans of Foreign Wars; a life member of the American Legion, the Association of the United States Army, and the Society of the First Infantry Division; and a Patriot Life Member (Benefactor) and board of directors member of the National Rifle Association. West was appointed by Texas Lt. Gov. Dan Patrick to the Texas Sunset Advisory Commission. He lives with his family in Dallas, Texas.